The Faith of the Psalmists

THE FAITH OF THE PSALMISTS

by HELMER RINGGREN

FORTRESS PRESS   PHILADELPHIA

This book is the author's own English version of his *Psaltarens Fromhet,* published in 1957 by the Svenska Kyrkans Diakonistyrelses Bokförlag in Stockholm, Sweden.

© 1963 by Fortress Press
Library of Congress Catalog number 63-7906
Printed in U.S.A.
UB 930

Preface

MODERN PSALM research has been primarily interested in the reconstruction of the cultic background of the Psalms. While this is an extremely important task, the exclusive concentration on it tends to obscure another aspect of the matter, namely, the religious experience expressed in these poems. This book, while recognizing the value of cultic research and utilizing its results, aims at an analysis of those deeper religious aspects of the Psalms.

The book represents an adaptation and revision of my earlier Swedish book on the same subject, *Psaltarens Fromhet*. In preparing the manuscript I have made use of my English notes for a series of lectures given at the Swedish Theological Institute in Jerusalem in 1955. But the book would not have been what it is, were it not for the invaluable help of Dr. Bernard Erling of Gustavus Adolphus College, St. Peter, Minnesota, whose understanding of the subject matter and good sense of American style have performed miracles with my English. I take the opportunity to express my profound gratitude to him.

Helmer Ringgren

Åbo, Finland
September, 1962

Contents

Introduction

To TRACE the history of the Psalms in the Christian church would be an interesting and illuminating task. Such a study would doubtless reveal much of the fascinating history of Christian life and piety, for which the Psalms have always had no small significance. It would show how people of different epochs found their own situation prefigured in the Psalms and how they made the words of the psalmists their own. It would also provide valuable information concerning the interpretation of the Psalms throughout the course of Christian history, how in various ways they have been adapted to meet the practical needs of the believers.

Scholarly interpretation of the Psalms has varied greatly during the last century. Many of the changes which have taken place in this respect merit careful investigation themselves in order to determine the extent to which they have been prompted by the spiritual and intellectual currents of the various periods. Such a study would be useful in bringing modern students of the Old Testament to exercise greater restraint in their claim finally to have found the true meaning of the Psalms. It would undoubtedly demonstrate that our own contemporary views too are influenced by the spiritual and cultural situation of our time and are based on assumptions no less questionable than those of earlier biblical scholars. It would incidentally be interesting to know whether the attention currently being given to the cultic aspects of Old Testament religion has any connection with the awakening interest in liturgy throughout the Protestant world.

The extensive materials from the ancient Near East which have been brought to light during the last fifty years have enabled us to understand many things better than was formerly possible. Yet the new philological and historical information has not enabled us to solve all the riddles in the Psalms by any means, not even with respect to ascertaining simply their "literal" meaning. Much less are we able to determine exactly the inner experience out of which they arose and the piety of those who wrote them.

However, the Psalms are so important an evidence of ancient Israelitic religious life that the attempt must be made to understand them, not simply in terms of their exterior form but also in terms of the faith and piety that is implicit in them. Despite the difficulties that obtain, we must make the effort to arrive at and describe the religious experience which finds expression in them. For if we have rightly understood the original function of the Psalms, they reflect—for the most part—the official pre-exilic religion of Israel, whereas the prophetic literature of the Old Testament, which in many respects is revolutionary, follows a different course of its own. Together with a growing number of Old Testament scholars we shall assume that most of the psalms are pre-exilic (though some are undeniably post-exilic) and that they are preserved in approximately their original form. The latter assumption might, of course, be questioned. It is possible, indeed, that a certain revision of some psalms has taken place, but in most cases it is impossible to discern at what point these changes were made. Thus the best we can do is simply analyze the Psalms in their present form, as we have them in our Bible.

But before dealing with our main subject, namely, the

piety represented by the Psalms, two preliminary matters must be discussed. We must first consider the relation between the Psalms and the cult of pre-exilic Israel; and we must then attempt to define the relation between cult and piety.

The cult was the original setting of most of the psalms. Agreement on this point is virtually unanimous, though there is some divergence of opinion as to precisely how many psalms are really cultic (used in public worship in the temple) and how many are not. Some scholars assume the number of noncultic psalms to be rather large, while others go so far as to deny altogether the existence of any psalms that are not in some sense cultic, having at least had as their *original* setting some cultic situation.

When we speak of cult in this connection we do not mean primarily the sacrifices prescribed in the laws of the Pentateuch. Rather we are referring to temple festivals of a different kind. Though the law gives us little information about them, we can reconstruct the nature of these festivals on the basis of certain psalms and analogous observances among neighboring peoples.

The two scholars primarily responsible for this new understanding of the Psalms are Hermann Gunkel and Sigmund Mowinckel. Gunkel's research marks the beginning of the modern study of the Psalms.[1] Before his time the Psalms were considered to be works of David which reflected certain episodes in his own life, or else—when the theory of Davidic authorship was abandoned—they were thought to reflect events either in the history of Israel as a whole or in the lives of certain individuals. According to this approach, the main task of psalm research consisted in seeking to determine the concrete situations in which the various psalms were written.

Gunkel observed that the psalms could be classified in certain categories or types, each of which had its specific features in style and content. He assumed that each type of psalm had originally a specific function, and this function had to do with certain ceremonies of the temple cult. A psalm of thanksgiving, for instance, was presumably written to accompany a sacrifice of thanksgiving. Such a psalm did not reflect a specific situation, but was meant for use by any individual who wanted to offer a thanksgiving sacrifice. Since it was written to meet the needs of many, it reflected that which was typical of the many situations in which thanksgiving was offered. Thus, according to Gunkel, the Psalms were written originally not for private use—as confessions of individuals—but for use in the regular cult in the temple. This, of course, would not preclude the possibility that a psalm conceived in terms of a particular situation could find use in the cult as well, particularly if it reflected an experience that was sufficiently typical.

Mowinckel based his research on Gunkel's results. But in looking for the function of the Psalms, Mowinckel did not confine himself merely to the sacrificial cult. Through a study of Babylonian and other Near Eastern cultures he was led to assume the existence in ancient Israel of cultic ceremonies other than sacrifices, and he went on to reconstruct these ceremonies on the basis of allusions in the psalms. His theory of the so-called "enthronement festival" probably was his most important contribution.[2] Observing that a number of psalms (Pss. 47, 93, and 95-100) referring to Yahweh (RSV: "the Lord") as King contain the expression "The Lord reigns" or "is King" (*Yahweh malak*), Mowinckel asserted that a similar expression had been used when an earthly king ascended the throne (II Kings 9:13: "Jehu is king") and that consequently the phrase "The Lord is King" should rather be rendered: "Yahweh *has become* King." Rejecting earlier attempts to interpret these psalms either against a historical background or in purely eschatological terms as referring to the coming kingdom of God, Mowinckel went on to investigate their principal motifs: the kingship of the Lord, the creation of the world, the defeat of the enemies, and the judgment of the nations. Following the clue suggested by the celebration of the New Year's festival in Babylon with Marduk in the leading role, Mowinckel insisted that these "enthronement psalms" can be understood only against a cultic background of a similar kind. In his investigation Mowinckel combined the insights gained from an inductive study of the psalms themselves with his use of the analogy of the Babylonian festival and its counterparts elsewhere and with the comparisons he made with the rabbinical traditions concerning the celebration of the New Year and the Feast of Tabernacles in post-exilic Judaism. As the result of these inquiries he concluded that there was in ancient Israel an annual celebration of Yahweh's enthronement as the King of the universe, and that the psalms in question were chanted during this festival. Though the phrase "The Lord reigns" did not occur expressly, the enthronement motif was nevertheless present in a number of psalms which Mowinckel therefore included within the scope of his investigation (at first Pss. 8, 24, 29, 46, 48, 50, 65; later also Pss. 68,[3] 75, 76, 82, 84, 85, 87, 118).

According to his theory, the enthronement festival is the great occasion on which, year by year, Yahweh makes all things new, repeating his original triumph over the primeval chaos in the creation of the world. All this is expressed in a ritual drama in which Yahweh also triumphs over the kings and nations of the earth, who are regarded as allies of the primeval chaos. Part of the celebration involved a procession in which the ark as the symbol of Yahweh's presence was carried in triumph to the sanctuary, where Yahweh was acclaimed anew as the universal King. Thus does Yahweh vindicate the faith of his chosen people; he sees to it that everything is set in order again, and he renews his covenant with his people and with the house of David as represented by the reigning king. In this way Yahweh shows that he is prepared to renew the fortunes of his people for the coming year. Mowinckel finds, moreover, that Israel's eschatological hopes as set forth in the prophetic writings are to be traced to the hopes expressed at the enthronement festival. The "Day of Yahweh" was originally the day of his enthronement. But when the hopes connected with that day—hopes for a good year—were frustrated, the aspirations of the people were projected into the future and connected with the day when Yahweh would ultimately prove himself to be the universal King.

Mowinckel's theory has been accepted in principle by several Old Testament scholars who have published commentaries on the Psalms.[4] The so-called Uppsala School[5] has further developed his theses by bringing the enthronement festival into a closer connection with the New Year's festival of Babylon and ancient Canaan and by elaborating what is called the "myth and ritual" pattern, which is thought to have been the basis of cult and religion throughout the ancient Near East. This is not the place to enter upon a detailed discussion of the theories of the Uppsala School. It may be that further research will prove them to be too extreme and in need of modification. What is essential from our point of view is the fact that these scholars agree with Mowinckel in their high estimate of the cult and its significance for the religious life of Israel.

On the other hand, there has also been severe criticism of Mowinckel's theory. It is argued that since there is no direct reference to an enthronement festival in the Old Testament, its existence is very doubtful. This, of course, is the old "argument from silence." But since Mowinckel's theory presupposes that the enthronement festival was not celebrated after the exile, it should not be expected that the laws which received their final form in this later period should contain references to a festival that was then no longer celebrated. As we shall see, however, there may be nonetheless some allusions to such a festival in the historical books. Mowinckel is, of course, fully aware of the fact that his judgment is based primarily on an interpretation of the psalms themselves in the light of comparative religion and that, consequently, his conclusions are valid only to the extent that they are able to provide the best available explanation for the psalms in question.

One other objection should be considered. In his introduction to the Psalms in the *Interpreter's Bible*, W. Stewart McCullough writes: " . . . the idea that the Hebrew God could in any real sense be enthroned annually was poor theology."[6] Every Israelite knew that the Lord was King eternally and therefore it would not make sense to enthrone him anew every year.

This objection reveals a certain misunderstanding of the nature of cultic celebration. The Jews are aware of the exodus from Egypt as a historical fact, and yet they are asked to consider themselves as delivered from Egypt at every Passover. Roman Catholics know that Jesus died on Calvary, and yet they believe that his vicarious sacrifice is repeated in every mass. Orthodox Christians know very well that the resurrection took place long ago and that Jesus lives, and yet they repeat the response every Easter night, "Christ is risen, indeed." A cultic, symbolical celebration of a historical (or mythological) fact does not minimize that fact, nor is it "poor theology": it is a way of reliving events that are of basic significance for faith.

The classification of a large number of psalms as belonging to a great annual festival is accepted by Artur Weiser in his commentary on the Psalms in *Das Alte Testament deutsch*.[7] However, instead of calling it an "enthronement festival"—

which in view of McCullough's remark is an unhappy expression—he prefers the term "covenant festival," because
the Old Testament alludes to a festival concerned with
renewal of the covenant and reaffirmation of the obligation
to keep the law (II Kings 23:1-3; cf. Deut. 31:10-13 and Josh.,
chap. 24, especially vs. 25). (Gerhard von Rad has connected
this ritual with the Feast of Tabernacles,[8] and Mowinckel
himself is inclined to regard the enthronement festival as an
aspect of the Feast of Tabernacles.)[9] Otherwise Weiser finds
approximately the same elements in the covenant festival as
Mowinckel does in his enthronement festival.

Another German scholar, Hans-Joachim Kraus, is more
critical of Mowinckel's theory. A brief discussion of his work
on the kingship of God in the Old Testament[10] may be of
some interest in this connection. Kraus criticizes Mowinckel
for making the category of the enthronement psalms too
inclusive. Strictly speaking, he says, only those psalms which
expressly mention God as King should be assigned to this
group, i.e., Pss. 47, 93, 96, 97, 98, 99. Kraus states further
that the enthronement festival is never mentioned in the Old
Testament, and it cannot be proved that there are even
allusions to it. Mowinckel's theory of a cultic drama in which
Yahweh's victory over his enemies was enacted is erroneous,
because it is impossible to dramatize in the cult the trembling
(quaking) of the earth (Pss. 96:9; 99:1) and the epiphany of
the God of Israel as described in these psalms.[11]

This critique, however, reveals Kraus's complete ignorance
of the character of cultic drama. Actually, the greatest events
may be intimated by very insignificant acts. The Greek Orthodox liturgy re-enacts the whole history of redemption. In
Egypt, for example, there was a ceremony at Edfu, enacting
the defeat of the powers of chaos in the shape of a terrible
hippopotamus, but in the cult this struggle was symbolized
by thrusting a knife into a small loaf![12] At a certain moment

in the Babylonian New Year's festival a dove was sliced open in order to symbolize how the chaos monster Tiamat was cut in half by Marduk, to be used later at the creation of the world.[13] In other words, we know nothing of the acts which might have symbolized the creation of the world and Yahweh's epiphany—they may have been very simple and insignificant in their outward form—but we do know their symbolical meaning as expounded in the Psalms.

After rejecting entirely the hypothesis of a pre-exilic enthronement festival, Kraus goes on to develop his own theory. He starts with the account of David's bringing up the ark to Zion (II Sam., chap. 6), an incident cited also by Mowinckel. Kraus finds that chapters 6 and 7 in II Samuel cannot be separated from each other and that these two chapters, relating the founding of the Jerusalem sanctuary, contain a story which must have been told to visiting pilgrims and repeatedly enacted in an annual festival. The principal ideas of this story are the election of Jerusalem and the election of David as king of Israel. These ideas are also expressed in Psalm 132, which is probably a hymn belonging to that festival. Similar ideas are found in the account of Solomon's dedication of the temple in I Kings, chapter 8 (notice vs. 16!), and there are further allusions to such a festival in I Kings 12:32, 33 (Jeroboam institutes a festival at Bethel "like that of Judah") and II Kings 23:1-3 (Josiah reads the law and renews the covenant). From these accounts Kraus draws the following conclusion: On the first day of the Feast of Tabernacles there was a "royal Zion festival" in Jerusalem, in which the election of Jerusalem and of the Davidic dynasty was proclaimed and celebrated. A procession in which the ark was carried to Zion and an installation of the dynasty were essential elements in this festival.

It is impossible, Kraus says, to combine the enthronement psalms with this festival. Instead, he mentions Pss. 132; 78:65-

72; 24:7-10; 2; 72; and the "Zion songs" in Pss. 84, 87, and 122 as belonging to the festival he reconstructs.

The enthronement psalms, on the other hand, are not pre-exilic, according to Kraus. The idea of Yahweh's universal kingship—not that of the Jerusalemite king—reveals the influence of Deutero-Isaiah, and the enthronement festival is therefore a post-exilic institution, partly eschatological in character. The dependence on Deutero-Isaiah in these psalms is proved by the great number of similar or identical phrases, as well as the similarity of ideas. As real enthronement psalms Kraus then lists Pss. 47, 93, 97, 99, 96, 98.

A discussion of the question of the priority of the enthronement or of Deutero-Isaiah is not possible at this point. It has been pointed out, however, by A. R. Johnson that calling attention to the parallels between Pss. 93, 96-98, and Isa., chaps. 40-55, may prove to be a two-edged sword, since the evidence may also support the opposite conclusion.[14] Thus the evidence cited may be used to show that dependence is really on the side of Deutero-Isaiah. In passing, it may also be mentioned that what Kraus says about the Uppsala School reveals that often he has not clearly understood its intentions. Nor is it a valid argument in a scholarly discussion to suggest, as Kraus at one point does, that, because certain findings, if true, are theologically dangerous, they must be false![15]

Apart from these shortcomings, Kraus's book contains some valuable observations, and his criticism of Mowinckel is in some respects probably justified. What should be noted, however, is the fact that not even Kraus, who is wholly opposed to Mowinckel and the Uppsala School, is able to abandon completely the cultic interpretation—of which they are the chief advocates.

If we maintain that the Psalms are our best source for an understanding of the religious life of ancient Israel, and that they do have a cultic setting, we must then ask ourselves: What is the relation between cult and religious life? This problem was dealt with by G. Quell in his study of the cultic problem in the Psalms.[16] The work appeared shortly after the publication of the first volumes of Mowinckel's *Psalmen-studien,* the results of which Quell accepts for the most part, at least as far as the cultic setting of the Psalms is concerned. It is obvious that Quell has become aware of the problem through Mowinckel's writings.

Asserting that in the synagogue the psalms were not used in the service, but only as material for teaching and edification, Quell holds that this is true also of those psalms which were originally cultic songs. Then he points out that it is always difficult to determine with certainty whether or not a psalm is cultic, i.e., written for use in the cult. This is due to what Quell calls "the formal monotony of the psalms,"[17] by which he means that the authors of the psalms felt obligated to express their thoughts in traditional words and formulas inherited from previous generations.

Though religious language is always conservative, it does not follow that the use of traditional forms reveals a lack of real religious experience in the authors of the psalms, or in those who used them in the cult. On the contrary, it often happens that well-known and stylized phrases are able to create, again and again, religious emotions in people who have become accustomed to them and who use them to express their own religious experience. This may be because such phrases recall earlier religious experiences and reactualize them.

The predilection of the psalmists for certain forms and expressions given by religious tradition, however, does cause serious difficulties when we try to define the nature of a psalm and to determine whether or not it is cultic. Owing to the stereotyped character of the style, phrases originally belonging to the cultic sphere may be used in noncultic connections in some psalms. This overlapping makes it very difficult, if not impossible, to learn anything about the personal experience behind the psalms or about the individual piety and personality of the author. Belonging to the sphere of suprapersonal religion, cult, says Quell, is not a personal, individual matter but the concern of the whole community. Cult is not only the result of religious experience; it also creates it anew.[18] While this observation is true, it is also true that the collective character of the cultic experience does not exclude individual experiences and emotions of the participants in the cult—a fact which Quell admits but does not sufficiently stress.

Quell goes on to attempt a definition of the concepts "cult" and "piety."[19] He mentions four characteristics of cult: (1) In cult we have to do with acts which can be observed with our senses, acts which can be seen and heard and are for the most part bound to a fixed time or place. (2) The different forms of cult emanate from piety and aim at expressing "pious"—that is to say, "religious"—experience. (3) Cult is a social phenomenon, a function of the community rather than of individual life—"one religious individual does not constitute a cult, it is only the congregation that can be a cultic subject"—which means that individual prayer would not be regarded as belonging to the cult. (4) Cult is organized; it is necessarily bound up with a clergy and a liturgy.

Citing the testimony of the prophets (Amos 5:21-24; Hos. 6:6; Isa. 1:10-17; Mic. 6:6-8), Quell holds that "piety"[20] is essentially different from cult. This does not mean, however, that the prophets wanted a religion without any form of cult whatsoever, for in their criticism they were referring only to perverted forms of cult. We must remember, says Quell, that the prophets were preaching to ordinary people and had to exaggerate their statements if they wanted to be understood at all.

Thus, according to Quell, there is a real and essential difference between cult and piety. One may agree with him that cult can become nothing but observance of external rites and ceremonies, void of religious content, and that the essence of piety is to be found in religious experience. But to postulate a basic and essential difference between cult and piety is illogical, for by Quell's own admission cult not only expresses piety but also creates and sustains it. There may be cultic acts which neither express nor strengthen the religious experience of specific individuals. There may even be a piety which has no relation to cult but is devoid of social implications. However, this seems very unlikely since religion is generally transmitted from generation to generation or from individual to individual through certain social acts, such as praying together, participating in religious ceremonies, and attending church services. Psychologically speaking, we may say that conversions are brought about by human influence of one kind or other. The social element of religion is rightly receiving much attention in modern psychology and sociology, for there is, as a matter of fact, continuous interaction between cult and religious experience. One does not exist without the other.

With respect to the Psalms and the piety expressed in them, it is obviously impossible to follow Quell in making such a sharp distinction between cult and piety or in saying that in a given instance the cultic elements actually hinder the growth of real piety. It is not fair to regard the psalmists as lacking in religious experience or personal piety on the grounds that they nourished their religious life with that which they experienced in the cult. Instead, we have to try to understand their religious experience in precisely this cultic setting. We must analyze it as it appears in the Psalms, and not judge it according to a standard alien to the Psalms themselves. In other words, we must analyze the religion of the Psalms as cultic religion, as piety nourished by the cult and expressed in cultic acts. It is even possible that many psalms which do not expressly mention the cult or cultic ceremonies actually belong to the cult nonetheless and should be judged as expressions of cultic piety rather than as private prayers expressing an individualistic religion without any social or cultic implications.

CHAPTER 1

The Cultic Element

THE RELIGION of the Psalms is cultic religion. The Psalms were not written for private use—at least, not originally—but for use in the cult of the Yahwistic community, and in most cases for the cult of the pre-exilic community. This fact accounts for the high estimation of the temple which appears in many psalms. "The Lord is in his holy temple" (Ps. 11:4); he dwells in the sanctuary (Pss. 26:8; 46:4; 74:2; 132:13 f.[1]); and he reveals himself in the temple to the congregation that has come together to celebrate a festival:

> Out of Zion, the perfection[2] of beauty,
> God shines forth.
> Our God comes, he does not keep silence,
> before him is a devouring fire,
> round about him a mighty tempest.
> —*Ps. 50:2,3*

> Honor and majesty are before him;
> strength and beauty are in his sanctuary.
> —*Ps. 96:6*

There has been much discussion concerning these passages and some related ones that refer to a theophany, or appearance of God, namely, Pss. 68:7 f.; 18:7-15; and 77:16 ff. The question is: To what does this description of God's appearance refer? Does it refer to a historical event, such as the giving of the law on Mount Sinai? Or does it refer to a ceremony performed in the cult and symbolizing Yahweh's coming forth to deliver his people? Many Old Testament scholars have accepted the latter theory. They hold that the events of Mount Sinai, the giving of the law and the covenant, were not only commemorated but also dramatized in some way, re-enacted in a cultic drama or represented in the form of symbolic actions. Weiser[3] assumes that these psalms reflect an essential part of the ceremonies connected with the covenant festival, while Kraus[4] is very skeptical at this point, and asks how such things could possibly have been represented ceremonially in the cult. He thinks that the geographical setting of the theophanies in Judges, chap. 5, and Psalm 68 speaks in favor of a historical interpretation. But, as has been indicated, Kraus's argument is not persuasive, since so little is needed to represent or symbolize a mythological event in the cult. Moreover, it should have been just as natural in ancient Israel to sing of Sinai as it is for Christians today to sing of Bethlehem at Christmas time. In the case of Psalm 50, it is even expressly stated that the Lord comes from Zion, i.e., from the sanctuary. What is meant is thus a glorious revelation of Yahweh, symbolized in the cultic observance. That being so, we can also understand more clearly the following passage:

> So I have looked upon thee in the sanctuary,
> beholding thy power and glory.[5]   —*Ps. 63:2*

Even if this should not refer to the cultic theophany, it shows clearly what the sanctuary meant to the pious Israelite: there he met God, seeing him in his power and glory. *Kabod*, "glory," as is well known, refers to something shining and brilliant connected with the occasions when God reveals himself to men (cf. Isa., chap. 6; Ezek., chaps. 1-3). It is not only his "glory" in general, but the light, the splendor around him. Some scholars think it was especially connected with the cultic theophany.[6]

On the basis of this interpretation we are also better prepared to understand other passages which refer to love for the sanctuary and to the joy experienced on being there, such as:

> I was glad when they said to me,
> "Let us go to the house of the Lord!"
> —Ps. 122:1

> One thing have I asked of the Lord,
> that will I seek after;
> that I may dwell in the house of the Lord
> all the days of my life,
> to behold the beauty of the Lord,[7]
> and to inquire in his temple. —Ps. 27:4

To "dwell in the house of the Lord" does not refer to permanent residence in the temple, since nobody lived in the sanctuary itself, but is probably an expression for the sojourn of the temple visitor at the holy place, where he is satiated by the spiritual richness of the encounter there with holiness.[8] The place is holy, because God is there present, and where God is present there is also to be found spiritual plenitude. It is more difficult to know what the original term for "to inquire" means. In Ezek. 34:11 f. it occurs together with darash, "to seek," and obviously means "to search," or the like. In II Kings 16:15 it refers to something that is done on the altar. Here it could possibly refer to a cultic act performed in order to obtain an oracle or a divine answer to a question. Other ancient peoples sought oracles through observing the intestines of sacrificial animals, but nothing similar is recorded as having occurred in Israel. It is possible that the asking of questions of Yahweh could have been accompanied by sacrifices. But it is also possible that the word is used in a more general sense: to meditate upon something, to consider, to reflect. It is conceivable that "to behold his beauty" refers to witnessing the ceremonies of the theophany in the temple, but it could perhaps also be taken in a metaphorical sense. In any case, this verse is a very good illustration of the significance of the temple for the pious man's relation to God: in the temple he experiences the nearness of God, possibly concretized also in familiar ceremonies and cultic objects. But what is more important to the psalmist than these outward things is the presence of God; the worshiper wants to "dwell" in the temple because God is there, and because he can behold God's "beauty" there. His conception of the cult is theocentric, God-centered.

In this connection we should remember Ps. 23:6 ("I shall dwell in the house of the Lord for ever") and Ps. 65:4:

> Blessed is he whom thou dost choose and bring near,
> to dwell in thy courts.[9]
> We shall be satisfied with the goodness of thy house,
> thy holy temple!

Because of the use of the verb "to be satisfied" it is probable that the term "goodness" contains an allusion to a sacrificial meal (cf. Jer. 31:14), although it is also possible that it refers more generally to all that is "good" and edifying, experienced during the visit to the temple (Gunkel).

A similar idea is developed in the following verses:

> They feast on the abundance of thy house,
> and thou givest them drink from the river of thy delights.
> For with thee is the fountain of life;
> in thy light do we see light.   —Ps. 36:8, 9

It has been suggested that the expression "take refuge in the shadow of thy wings" in Ps. 36:7 alludes to the wings of the cherubim on the ark in the temple, which would be another allusion to the cult; but we may leave this question open. It is obvious, however, that vss. 8,9 must refer to a

4

ceremony in the temple, probably a sacrificial act, for word that is rendered by the RSV as "abundance" mean. literally "fatness" and refers to the fat of the sacrificial animals. The important thing, however, is that it is not the ceremony in itself that is emphasized but the communion with God experienced in the cultic act. The sacrificial meal becomes a token of God's presence and of the worshiper's communion with him. "The temple service is the bridge between God and man," as Weiser says. The "light" referred to in vs. 9 might be God's *kabod* or "glory," a sign of his presence and a token of his grace, which means life full and rich for the believer.[10]

Psalm 5 contains a prayer, in which the psalmist first expresses his conviction that his enemies, the wicked and boastful ones, shall not stand before God because they are an abomination to him. Then he goes on to say:

> But I through the abundance of thy steadfast love
> will enter thy house,
> I will worship toward thy holy temple
> in the fear of thee.   —*Ps. 5:7*[11]

Going to the temple to prostrate oneself before the place where the Lord dwells is set over against the separation of the wicked from God. Worshiping in the sanctuary is the positive value refused to those whom the Lord "abhors" (Ps. 5:6) but granted to the psalmist through God's "steadfast love."

Another instance of the role played by the temple and the cult is found in the following words:

> I wash my hands in innocence,
> and go about thy altar, O Lord.
> . . . .
> O Lord, I love the habitation of thy house,
> and the place where thy glory dwells.
>   —*Ps. 26:6, 8*

This obviously refers to some kind of procession in the temple service. The washing of the hands represents a ceremony of purification which prepares one to partake in the procession round the altar. Again there is a reference to God's *kabod* or "glory" as dwelling in the temple.

There are two psalms which in their entirety bear witness to the significance of the temple for the faith of the psalmists. One of them is the well-known Psalm 42-43 (obviously these two were originally *one* psalm), which compares the longing of the soul for God with that of the thirsty hart for water. As the following verses indicate, this psalm expresses the psalmist's longing for the temple and the cult:

> My soul thirsts for God,
> for the living God.
> When shall I come and behold
> for the living God.
>
> . . . .
>
> These things I remember,
> as I pour out my soul:
> how I went with the throng,[12]
> and led them in procession to the house of God,
> with glad shouts and songs of thanksgiving,
> a multitude keeping festival.   —*Ps. 42:2,4*

To "behold the face of God" is simply to visit the temple. The psalmist's question is: When shall I be able to visit God's sanctuary again? God is in the temple; the psalmist is longing to "behold" him there and to partake in the ceremonies of the cult (Ps. 42:5). But for some reason he is obviously unable to go to the temple and participate in the cult. He is excluded from the cultic community. The reason is difficult to determine. According to the commonly accepted view, he is exiled in the northern part of Galilee at the sources of the Jordan River near Mount Hermon (see Ps. 42:6), but this geographical interpretation is by no means certain. Since the next verse uses such terms as *tehom* ("deep calls to deep")

6

and waves and billows, which otherwise refer to the waters of Sheol, it is possible that vs. 6 also should be taken in a figurative sense. In that case the whole passage would refer only to the suffering and anxiety of the psalmist, as he feels himself overwhelmed by the forces of death and Sheol, abandoned by his God and remote from him. But whatever one's conclusion with respect to these details, it is clear enough that the psalm expresses love and longing for the temple as the place where God dwells. This is apparent in the two first verses of Psalm 42, which expressly mention God as the object of the psalmist's thirst and desire, while the context makes it clear that God is regarded as dwelling in his sanctuary.

Therefore the psalmist prays in Ps. 43:3,4:

> Oh send out thy light and thy truth;
> let them lead me,
> let them bring me to thy holy hill
> and to thy dwelling!
> Then I will go to the altar of God,
> to God my exceeding joy.

Again we notice the close association of the altar with God, so that the two are made almost synonymous. On the temple altar God is present in a special way. Yet this psalm also shows that it is possible to pray to God elsewhere than in the temple. It would be unfair to dismiss this psalm as an expression of external religion simply because of its high appreciation of the cult. The cult and the temple have been for the psalmist a source of strength and religious life from which he has gotten help in hours of struggle and distress. "No religion could do without a cult as the place where man again and again receives new power for the struggle of life through fellowship with God and with other believers" (Weiser).

The other psalm that speaks of the temple is Psalm 84:

7

> How lovely is thy dwelling place, O Lord of hosts!
> My soul longs, yea, faints for the courts of the Lord;
> my heart and flesh sing for joy to the living God.[13]
> —*Ps. 84:1,2*

Quell, who interprets the word "lovely" as reflecting an aesthetic or at least a "predominantly aesthetic" experience of the author of this psalm, is certainly in error.[14] J. Steinmann[15] comes closer to the truth when he points out that the words *yadid*, "lovely," and *niksaph*, "to long," belong to the language of love. He recalls the frequent use in mysticism of expressions and images from the sphere of love. "The view of Jerusalem produces an almost sensual desire for the life that has its source in God," he says, adding that it is certainly a mystical fervor that burns in the psalmist.[16] We notice that in vs. 2 "the courts of the Lord" and "the living God" are parallel and consequently more or less equivalent. Furthermore, the expression "my heart and my flesh" designates man as a totality; his entire person, body and soul, is engaged in this religious experience.

The next verses use a figure of speech that is well known also in Sumerian and Babylonian psalms, expressing the security felt in God's sanctuary:

> Even the sparrow finds a home,
> and the swallow a nest for herself,
> where she may lay her young,
> at thy altars, O Lord of hosts,
> my king and my God.
> . . . .
> Blessed are the men whose strength is in thee,
> in whose hearts are the highways [to Zion].
> —*Ps. 84:3, 5*

The "highways" ("Zion," as the RSV indicates, is not in the Hebrew text) are either the roads leading to the temple, or possibly the processional roads. In any case, the context shows that having one's strength in God is linked up with taking part in the temple service:

> They go from strength to strength;
> the God of gods will be seen in Zion.
> . . . .
> For a day in thy courts is better
> than a thousand [elsewhere].[17]
> I would rather be a doorkeeper in the house of my God
> than dwell in the tents of wickedness.   —*Ps. 84:7,10*

Verse 7 is not quite clear. It has been suggested that instead of going "from strength to strength" the reference should rather be to going "from rampart to rampart" until the pilgrims finally reach the holy city and the temple. Be that as it may, it seems possible that in the second line, where the Hebrew text is ambiguous, the old Greek translation may be correct: "until they see the God of gods on Zion." But whichever reading we prefer, the great significance of the temple service for strengthening the faith of the worshipers is obvious. In vs. 10 the psalmist's thoughts are directed to everyday life, and we sense a fear that the strength derived from the cult may be weakened and even dissipated, should he have to dwell far from the temple.

It would be easy to cite more instances of the prominent role of the temple in Israelitic religion. We shall mention only one more example, Psalm 122, from which a verse has already been quoted. The psalm is a hymn in praise of Jerusalem as the holy city of the Lord, the city "to which the tribes go up . . . to give thanks to the name of the Lord." Here too the language of love is used: "May they prosper who love you!" It would be difficult to account for this great significance of the temple if the cult performed there had been exclusively the sacrificial cult referred to in the law. The Psalms, of course, do mention sacrifices of various kinds (Pss. 4:5; 20:3; 27:6; 50:5; 54:6; 56:12; 66:13; 96:8).[18] A study

9

of these passages shows that sacrifices are generally referred to as something quite natural. They are offered as a token of gratitude with great joy (especially Ps. 27:6), and they express trust in God (Ps. 4:5). It should not be forgotten that sacrifices were regarded as a channel of divine grace and a means of fellowship between man and God.[19]

But there is also criticism of the sacrificial cult. In Psalm 50, for instance, God addresses the congregation in the following way:

> I will accept no bull from your house,
> nor he-goat from your folds.
> For every beast of the forest is mine,
> the cattle on a thousand hills.
> I know all the birds of the air,
> and all that moves in the field is mine.
> . . . .
> Do I eat the flesh of bulls,
> or drink the blood of goats?
> Offer to God a sacrifice of thanksgiving,
> and pay your vows to the Most High.
> —Ps. 50:9-11,13,14

It is easy to understand why these words have often been taken as an absolute rejection of sacrifices. But if we read vs. 5 of the same psalm, we find that sacrifices are not rejected at all, but are mentioned as a necessary element in the making of a covenant. And in vs. 8 we read:

> I do not reprove you for your sacrifices;
> your burnt offerings are continually before me.
> —Ps. 50:8

Obviously the point is that all sacrificial animals are, in fact, already God's property. Man is not able to give anything to God that is not already His. Sacrifices must therefore be offered with the proper sense of gratitude and "thanksgiving" (vs. 14), in recognition that everything comes from God as his gracious gift to mankind, so that what men give to God does not add to his possessions. "For all things come from thee, and of thy own have we given thee" (I Chron. 29:14). It should be noted that Psalm 50 begins with a description of a theophany that takes place in Zion. The psalm consequently has an intimate relation to the temple cult.

Our next passage, Ps. 40:6-8, seems to be entirely negative in its attitude to sacrifice:

> Sacrifice and offering thou dost not desire;
> but thou hast given me an open ear.
> Burnt offering and sin offering
> thou hast not required.
> Then I said, "Lo, I come;
> in the roll of the book it is written of me;
> I delight to do thy will, O my God;
> thy law is within my heart."

The psalmist says: *Not* sacrifice *but* doing God's will. Yet this should probably be interpreted as an example of the Hebrew way of expressing things, so to speak, in black and white instead of defining the exact shade of color. The meaning is obviously that doing God's will is more important than sacrifice, and that sacrifices without obedience are worthless.[20] But the psalmist has certainly not intended the abolition of the sacrificial service, nor even conceived of the possibility of a religion without sacrifices and cultic performances. Verses 9 and 10 seem to indicate that the psalm was recited in the temple: the "great congregation" (*qahal rab*) is the cult congregation of Yahweh. Probably the meaning would be clearer to us if we were able to ascertain the original function of the psalm. Weiser thinks that it belonged to the covenant festival and that in ancient Israel the "covenant cult" was held to be more important than the sacrificial cult. According to him, the point of the verses quoted is that it is not the sacrificial cult, but the covenant cult that is essential. In other words, the annual renewal of the covenant with the obligation of ful-

11

filling the commandments of the law as the foundation of the covenant was more important than regular sacrifice.

There are comparable passages which may be mentioned:

> For thou hast no delight in sacrifice;
> were I to give a burnt offering, thou wouldst not be pleased.
> The sacrifice acceptable to God is a broken spirit;
> a broken and contrite heart, O God, thou wilt not despise.
> —*Ps. 51:16,17*

It has been suggested that the reason for God's rejecting sacrifices is the fact that the temple is in ruins, for vss. 19 ff. say that God will receive right sacrifices when the walls of Jerusalem have been rebuilt.[21] But it is also possible that these two verses are a later addition to the psalm, which in itself is certainly pre-exilic. At any rate, the verses quoted represent a spiritualization of the idea of sacrifice: a broken spirit, repentance, is more acceptable to God than sacrifices, and can even replace sacrifices.

Other similar passages are:

> Let my prayer be counted as incense before thee,
> and the lifting up of my hands as an evening sacrifice!
> —*Ps. 141:2*

> And I will offer in his tent
> sacrifices with shouts of joy;
> I will sing and make melody to the Lord.
> —*Ps. 27:6*

> I will praise the name of God with a song;
> I will magnify him with thanksgiving.
> This will please the Lord more than an ox
> or a bull with horns and hoofs.
> —*Ps. 69:30,31*

> And let them offer sacrifices of thanksgiving,
> and tell of his deeds in songs of joy!
> —*Ps. 107:22*

> I will offer to thee the sacrifice of thanksgiving
> and call on the name of the Lord.
> —*Ps. 116:17*

In the first of these passages it is obvious that pra
pared with the pleasant odor of the sacrifice of inc
this does not mean that prayer should replace sacri
the contrary, both are good. In the second passage it
clear whether the shout of joy is to be counted as a sacri.   or
is to accompany the sacrificial acts, though the latter is more
probable. In the last two passages there is some ambiguity that
is not recognizable in the English translation. The word for
"sacrifice of thanksgiving," *todah*, can also mean "thanks" or
"thanksgiving"; consequently, the reference could also be
to thanksgiving as a sort of offering. One thing, however,
should be remembered in this connection: this spiritualized
interpretation of sacrifices could very well exist alongside the
traditional sacrifices.[22] Praise, thanksgiving, and repentance
did not replace sacrifices in the period with which we are
dealing.

But it would seem that sacrifices were not the only and
perhaps not even the most important cultic acts in pre-exilic
Israel. The Psalms allude to quite a number of other ceremonies. We have mentioned the allusion to a procession in
Psalm 42. There is probably another such allusion in Ps.
118:27:

> Bind the festal procession with branches,
> up to the horns of the altar!

The exact interpretation of the verse is not clear. In the
original Hebrew the three words that form the first line can
all have more than one connotation.[23] But the verse must, in
any case, refer to some cultic act or ceremony in the temple.
In Psalm 68 there is a vivid description of a procession in the
temple:

> Thy solemn processions are seen, O God,
> the processions of my God, my King, into the sanctuary—
> the singers in front, the minstrels last,
> between them maidens playing timbrels. —*Ps. 68:24,25*

13

The next verse tells us the purpose of the procession: it is to praise God:

"Bless God in the great congregation,
the Lord, O you who are of Israel's fountain!"
—*Ps. 68:26*

Dancing is mentioned in Ps. 149:3:

Let them praise his name with dancing,
making melody to him with timbrel and lyre!

In all these cases it is clear from the context that processions and dancing are not valuable in themselves; they are only means of praising God.

There is also a description of temple music in Psalm 81:

Sing aloud to God our strength;
shout for joy[24] to the God of Jacob!
Raise a song, sound the timbrel,
the sweet lyre with the harp.
Blow the trumpet at the new moon,
at the full moon, on our feast day.
For it is a statute for Israel,
an ordinance of the God of Jacob.
—*Ps. 81:1-4*

Quell is certainly right in saying that the piety which pervades this psalm emanates from the cultic jubilation at a great festival[25] in the temple. The cultic jubilation is prescribed by God as "a statute for Israel." But it is hard to follow Quell when he says that the religious element, or "piety," is found only in vss. 6 ff., while the introductory verses express the idea that the cult is an *opus operatum,* an act effective in itself.[26] It is difficult to understand why it must be regarded as an *opus operatum* to praise God by remembering his redemptive deeds of long ago when he delivered his people out of Egypt (vs. 5). The psalm goes on to call the people to repent and to enter again into the duties of the covenant. Thus the festival includes a renewal of the covenant, in which the people take upon themselves anew the duties of the law. This can hardly be called an *opus operatum*.

We need not here discuss all the allusions to cultic ceremonies in the Psalms. We shall therefore only mention in passing such interesting details as: the purification with hyssop in Ps. 51:7, the washing of the hands in Ps. 26:6 (perhaps also in Ps. 51:2,7), and the allusion to a cup in Ps. 116:13 which help us to realize that the worship in the temple was much richer than the prescriptions of the law would otherwise indicate.

The instances adduced so far have mentioned the temple and certain ceremonies performed in it, but there has been no allusion to a cultic drama of the kind assumed by Mowinckel. As a matter of fact, many scholars doubt that any such allusions are to be found. Mowinckel himself refers to a few passages,[27] but their demonstrative value has been contested by others. However, the possibility that these passages refer to some symbolical actions in the temple service should not be entirely ruled out.

Discussion of the passages is certainly justified:

> Come and see what God has done:
> he is terrible in his deeds among men.
> —*Ps. 66:5*

What is it that the hearers are invited to see? Obviously that which is mentioned in vs. 6: "He turned the sea into dry land; men passed through the river on foot. There did we rejoice in him."[28] Similarly in Ps. 46:8:

> Come, behold the works of the Lord,
> how he has wrought desolations in the earth.

This thought is again developed in Ps. 46:9:

> He makes wars cease to the end of the earth;
> he breaks the bow, and shatters the spear,
> he burns the chariots with fire!

15

It should perhaps be pointed out that Ps. 46:4 contains a clear allusion to the sanctuary, "the holy habitation of the Most High." The whole psalm has clearly the character of a psalm belonging to the great annual festival. Furthermore, we read in Ps. 48:8:

> As we have heard, so have we seen
> in the city of the Lord of hosts,
> in the city of our God,
> which God establishes for ever.

Again, Ps. 48:1,2 contains clear allusions to Zion and the temple. Verse 4 mentions kings who assembled against the Lord and his people, but were beaten back through divine intervention—exactly in the same manner as in the well-known royal psalm, Psalm 2. This might, of course, be taken as a reference to a historical event—although we hardly know of any situation that would suit the description—but it can also be understood as an allusion to a symbolic or dramatic representation of God's victory over his enemies. Also, the ships of Tarshish of Ps. 48:7 represent these enemies. The emphasis is not on the unique historical event, but on the theological or metaphysical and the wondrous nature of the divine activity (Weiser).

The congregation's reaction to that which they had seen is brought out in vss. 9 ff.:

> We have thought on thy steadfast love, O God,
> in the midst of thy temple.
> As thy name, O God,
> so thy praise reaches to the ends of the earth.
> Thy right hand is filled with victory;
> let Mount Zion be glad!
> Let the daughters of Judah rejoice because of thy judgments!
> —*Ps. 48:9-11*

Then there is a reference to some kind of procession around Zion in vs. 12, and finally the psalmist confesses in vs. 14:

> ... this is God,
> our God for ever and ever.
> He will be our guide for ever.

If we have interpreted the first part of the psalm correctly, as referring to a cultic ceremony, the second part, beginning with vs. 9, portrays the reaction of the community: seeing God's deeds prompts meditation on God's *chesed*, his loyalty and faithfulness with regard to the covenant. As was pointed out by Pedersen, "to remember a thing"—or, as here, "pondering over it"—means that it becomes an active reality in the life of the believer.[29] The cultic experience actualizes God's *chesed*. Accordingly, there is the singing of his praise (vs. 10a), rejoicing, and gladness in Jerusalem and the villages ("daughters") of Judah. This experience, finally, was to be passed on to coming generations. The participants in the procession were to look at the walls of the holy city (or the temple?), so that they could tell of their experience to the next generation. At the same time it is also probable that the procession was intended to confer the blessing of the festival—God's blessing —on the walls and the city.

This psalm, in any case, tells us something of the psychological effect of a great festival on the participants, of the rejoicing, enthusiasm, and deep gratitude called forth by that which the cultic performance actualized. Whatever position we take on the question of cultic drama, we have to admit, on the basis of the passages discussed, that something must have taken place in the cult which could be described by some participants at least as "seeing God's mighty deeds." They had an experience in the temple that could not be described appropriately otherwise than by using such verbs as "to see" and "to behold." This experience filled them with joy and happiness and gratitude. In other words, it strengthened their religious life and was a source of inspiration.

Therefore another psalmist says, in Ps. 118:24:

> This is the day which the Lord has made;[30]
> let us rejoice and be glad in it.

Or, to quote two enthronement psalms, in which praise and adoration are prevalent:

> O come, let us sing to the Lord;
> let us make a joyful noise[31] to the rock of our salvation!
> Let us come into his presence with thanksgiving;
> let us make a joyful noise to him with songs of praise!
> For the Lord is a great God,
> and a great King above all gods.
> . . . .
> O come, let us worship and bow down,
> let us kneel before the Lord, our Maker! —*Ps. 95:1-3,6*

> > Serve the Lord with gladness!
> > Come into his presence with singing!
> > . . . .
> > Enter his gates with thanksgiving,
> > and his courts with praise!
> > Give thanks to him, bless his name!
> > —*Ps. 100:2,4*

In both cases it is clear that the reference is to songs of praise in the temple and that the whole congregation is participating.

What the temple and temple service could mean to the pious Israelite in a situation of religious crisis is shown in Psalm 73. Many details in this psalm are obscure, but the general meaning is clear. The psalmist is struggling with the problem of the prosperity of the wicked and the suffering of the righteous, and he finds the solution in his fellowship with God. The turning point of the psalm comes when the psalmist visits the temple (Ps. 73:17: "until I went into the sanctuary of God"). There he learns for a certainty that God's enemies will finally be destroyed. We are not told how this certainty is gained, but in the light of what has been said it may be assumed that in some way he "sees the works of the Lord." If this is so, it is an excellent example of the significance of the cult in strengthening the faith of the worshiper.

This is not the place to discuss whether or not an enthronement festival (or "covenant festival," or New Year's festival) was celebrated in ancient Israel. But it must be stressed that even if these theories can and perhaps should be modified in many details, they have at least called our attention to an important fact, namely, the extraordinary significance of the cult in the religious life of ancient Israel, as reflected in the Psalms. It is very probable that there were cultic ceremonies, in which the Lord was celebrated as the Creator, the King, and the Judge of the world, and that the mythological or historical events connected with these concepts were symbolically represented or enacted in some way. It is almost universally recognized that there was an annual renewal of the covenant within a cultic framework, and it is likely that these ceremonies included some representation of the Sinai event.

But even if opinions may differ on many points, our investigation has shown that the significance of the temple worship for the religious life of Israel is not adequately described by the statement that the cult is an obstacle to piety.

CHAPTER 2

A Religion of Fellowship

THE RELIGION of the Psalms, in addition to being a cultic religion, is a religion of fellowship and communion. It seems advisable to avoid the adjective "collective," because it might give the impression that a personal or individual experience of God was absent. The religion of the Old Testament cannot easily be described as "individual" or "collective." There are individuals who are not simply parts of a collective whole, but who stand out as great religious personalities. On the other hand, there is the principle of collective responsibility and collective retribution: God punishes a whole community for the sins of an individual, or sons for the sins of their fathers. There is no simple formula to express at this point the rich variety of Israelitic social and religious life.

We are not going to discuss here, however, the question of collective versus individual religion.[1] We prefer to regard the individual's religion as a function of the worshiping community, as piety nourished by the believer's fellowship with other believers, that is, with other worshipers of the same God in the cult community of Israel. Thus the fact is not crucial that in a great number of psalms it is a collective—the people, the nation, or the community—that is the speaking subject, or that sometimes it is an individual who speaks in the name of the people; it simply bears witness to the feeling of fellowship and mutual dependence that pervades the Psalms. The individual, for example, who laments before God over his misery and suffering feels so connected with his fellow citizens that he expresses his vow of thanksgiving in the following form:

> Then I will thank thee in the great congregation;
> in the mighty throng I will praise thee.—*Ps. 35:18*

Or:

> I will tell of thy name to my brethren;
> in the midst of the congregation I will praise thee:
> . . . .
> From thee comes my praise in the great congregation;
> my vows I will pay before those who fear him.
> —*Ps. 22:22,25*

The "great congregation" (*qahal rab*) is Yahweh's cult congregation, or cult community. The psalmist does not want to appear before God alone; he wants to pay his vows in fellowship and communion with his brethren in the congregation. He wants to give thanks to God in their presence and tell them of the help that God has given him. God's gracious help is not a private matter; it concerns not only the individual, but the whole congregation.

Similar expressions occur rather frequently:

> I will thank thee for ever,
> because thou hast done it.
> I will proclaim thy name, for it is good,
> in the presence of the godly.   —*Ps. 52:9*

Or:

> My foot stands on level ground;
> in the great congregation I will bless the Lord.
> —*Ps. 26:12*

There is a similar note in Psalm 40:

> I have told the glad news of deliverance
> in the great congregation,
> lo, I have not restrained my lips,
> as thou knowest, O Lord.
> I have not hid thy saving help within my heart,
> I have spoken of thy faithfulness and thy salvation;
> I have not concealed thy steadfast love and thy faithfulness
> from the great congregation. —*Ps. 40:9,10*[2]

The reference here is to God's help and victory, his intervening to set things right, as recounted in the preceding verses of the psalm. His steadfast love (*chesed*) and his faithfulness have become manifest in his help and "salvation." But this divine help is no private matter; it is glad news that is to be told to the great congregation—and this is true whether the subject of the psalm is a king or an ordinary man.

It is only another aspect of the same attitude when the congregation is asked to participate in the praise of God which the psalmist is singing because of his salvation:

> Sing praises to the Lord, O you his saints,
> and give thanks to his holy name.
> —*Ps. 30:4*

It is obvious that the reason for this exhortation is the individual's experience of God's help and grace as described in vss. 1-3. The psalmist's thanksgiving concerns not only himself, but the whole congregation.

We may safely assume on the basis of these and similar passages that the temple cult played a very significant role in creating a feeling of intimate fellowship and communion among the people of Israel. In all likelihood the great festivals contributed much toward welding the people together religiously and nationally. The religious unity experienced at the central sanctuary had consequences also for the national unification of Israel.[3] As a matter of fact, these two aspects can be separated only in theory. The significance of the temple and the cult and especially of the great festivals in building up and maintaining national and religious unity can hardly be overestimated.

The emphasis is being shifted only slightly, therefore, when another psalmist says that he wants "to rejoice in the gladness of thy nation" and "glory with thy heritage" (Ps. 106:5). While the emphasis is here on the national aspect, the religious aspect is not absent, since the people stand before God as *his* people and *his* inheritance. Therefore we heartily agree with Otto J. Baab, when he says: "In the use of this literature [the Psalms] the individual became one with his group and shared the spirit which moved it, whether the mood of the moment was contrition, trust, or glad thanksgiving. He found himself, and he also found the God of his soul's desire through his unreserved participation in the acts of communal worship, whereby the rich resources and inspiring traditions of his people's history were made available to him."[4]

The negative aspect of this feeling of fellowship is encountered in the numerous passages where the psalmist complains of being abandoned by his friends and relatives:[5]

> I am the scorn of all my adversaries,
> a horror to my neighbors,
> an object of dread to my acquaintances;
> those who see me in the street flee from me.
> I have passed out of mind like one who is dead;
> I have become like a broken vessel. —*Ps. 31:11,12*

The misfortune of the psalmist isolates him from his neighbors and friends, for they consider him a sinful man, stricken by God, a man with whom people may not enter into normal fellowship. It follows that he is naturally excluded also from the cult community.[6]

In Psalm 35 we find a man who in the time of his prosperity shared the sorrows and needs of his fellow men, but now, when calamity has hit him, he feels abandoned by them all (see especially Ps. 35:11-16). There is another example in Psalm 88:

> Thou hast caused my companions to shun me;
> thou hast made me a thing of horror to them.
> I am shut in so that I cannot escape.
>
> ....
>
> Thou hast caused lover and friend to shun me;
> my companions are in darkness.   —*Ps. 88:8,18*

This psalm presents a special problem in that it is extremely difficult to determine its original setting. It is clear that it belongs to the category of laments, but there is a considerable variety of opinion concerning the actual situation involved. Some suggest illness[7] and characterize the psalmist as a man who from the days of his youth has been marked with suffering. Others believe that the psalm is a "prayer of an accused one."[8] Still others make the subject of the psalm the king, thinking that the psalm belongs to that part of the New Year's festival in which the king was humiliated and even thought to descend into the realm of death,[9] though, as has been indicated, the very existence of such a rite in Israel is questioned by many. From our point of view, however, it is clear that the grief and distress of the psalmist are increased by the fact that his friends and acquaintances avoid him, so that he is deprived of the fellowship and communion of those who should normally be most closely related to him. This is not only a social fact; it is also of religious importance, since it means that the poor man is deprived of the normal background of the worshiping congregation as he prays.

Another psalmist complains:

> Even my bosom friend in whom I trusted,
> who ate of my bread, has lifted his heel against me.
>   —*Ps. 41:9*

The last words of the verse are somewhat obscure, but they obviously denote a hostile act committed against the psalmist

—an act performed by a man who earlier had been very close to him as his "man of peace" (*ish shalom*; RSV: "my bosom friend") and with whom he had had a harmonious and unbroken relationship. This close relationship is further emphasized through reference to the sharing of meals: he who "ate of my bread." In this verse, therefore, the emphasis is obviously on the social aspect of the problem. The following passage emphasizes the religious aspect:

> It is not an enemy who taunts me—
> then I could bear it;
> it is not an adversary who deals insolently with me—
> then I could hide from him.
> But it is you, my equal,
> my companion, my familiar friend.
> We used to hold sweet converse together;
> within God's house we walked in fellowship.
> —*Ps. 55:12-14*

In the fellowship of the cult community the pious man experiences communion with God—only then does he experience it in full measure—and that is why such great distress is involved in the fact that a fellow worshiper breaks off fellowship, for thus he increases the psalmist's feeling of being abandoned by God. To be placed outside the cult community means to be excluded from the sphere within which God reveals himself without restriction. The outcast is not able fully to experience God's nearness and fellowship.

Every disturbance of the "peace" or "harmony" (*shalom*) which holds the community together implies a disturbance also of the individual's relation to his God, for when the individual is excluded from the cult community he is unable to fulfill adequately his religious function.

Mystics and hermits may praise solitude as a means of reaching an experience of God's grace and fellowship, but the pious Israelite does not feel that way about it. To him solitude or isolation is an evil, since it is primarily in the congregation that he experiences fellowship with his God. Some well-known lines of Psalm 102 use the image of lonely birds in the desert to describe the psalmist's solitude and misfortune:

> I am like a vulture of the wilderness,
> like an owl of the waste places;
> I lie awake,
> I am like a lonely bird on the housetop.
> —*Ps. 102:6,7*

It may be difficult to determine with scientific exactitude the species of the birds referred to. But the meaning of the passage is obviously that these birds normally belong to a flock; a lonely bird is an unfortunate being.[10] Similarly, a man who does not enjoy the fellowship of his neighbors is unable to lead a normal life either socially or religiously, for fellowship is one of the things that make life worth living. Consequently, the loneliness of the psalmist becomes a reason for God's intervention: "Turn to me, and be gracious to me; for I am lonely and afflicted" (Ps. 25:16). The psalmist needs divine aid because he lacks the normal sources of help that are to be found in fellowship with other men.

CHAPTER 3

Theocentric Religion

AN IMPORTANT feature of the religion of the Psalms is its theocentric or God-centered character. It is God and not man who is the focus of the psalmist's interest. This does not mean that human concerns are ignored, but they are, for the most part, subordinated to divine purposes. The theocentric attitude is not at all points consistently affirmed. Sometimes it must assert itself in competition with an anthropocentric or man-centered attitude. But a strong theocentric tendency is nonetheless present, even if at times it can only be detected by reading between the lines. The main concern in the Psalms is not the welfare of the psalmist, but the glory of God. God deals with man, and man calls for God's attention, but the ultimate purpose in both cases is the advancement of God's glory.

This is true not only of the hymns of praise, in which God's majesty and mighty deeds are praised, or of the psalms of thanksgiving, in which the psalmist acknowledges some happy event or some deliverance from danger and distress as God's work and expresses his gratitude for it. It is also true of many psalms of lament, in which the psalmist asks for deliverance from some actual suffering, for here the emphasis is often laid not on the deliverance as such, but solely on the glory of God:

> . . . call upon me in the day of trouble;
> I will deliver you, and you shall glorify me.
> —*Ps. 50:15*

Even if the misfortunes of the psalmist are often explained as the work of enemies—be they sorcerers or other personal enemies or national enemies[1]—it is equally often said that the suffering comes from God as a sign of his wrath: "For day and night *thy* hand was heavy upon me" (Ps. 32:4). "Wilt *thou* be angry with us for ever? Wilt *thou* prolong *thy* anger to all generations?" (Ps. 85:5). "*Thou* hast renounced the covenant with thy servant; *thou* hast defiled his crown in the dust" (Ps. 89:39).

Still more important, however, is the fact that in spite of all his suffering, in spite of his being punished, in spite of his sense of being abandoned by God, the psalmist feels bound to God. Even if he is tormented—be it by the enemies or by the wrath of God—he holds fast to God. It never occurs to him to turn away from God and his grace and goodness, or to deny his power. On the contrary, the psalmist knows that his only escape is to turn to God. It is only fools who say in their hearts: " 'There is no God' " (Ps. 14:1). It is only the "wicked" (*reshaim*) who say: " 'How can God know? Is there knowledge in the Most High?' " (Ps. 73:11). It is a dull and stupid man who does not know or understand God's marvelous works (Ps. 92:6). Even when the psalmist feels abandoned by God, he does not turn away from God, but cries out to him for help: "My God, my God, why hast thou forsaken me?" (Ps. 22:1).

> Hide not thy face from me,
> Turn not thy servant away in anger,
> thou who hast been my help.
> Cast me not off, forsake me not,
> O God of my salvation!   —*Ps. 27:9*

I had said in my alarm,
"I am driven far from thy sight."
But thou didst hear my supplications,
when I cried to thee for help.—*Ps. 31:22*

The pious man in the Psalms cannot escape his God; he cannot avoid seeing in God his only refuge, even if his own plight leads him to doubt the goodness and power of God. "Nevertheless I am continually with thee" (Ps. 73:23).

When an unfortunate man in his distress cries out for help and deliverance, he may naturally refer to his own sad plight as the occasion for God's compassion, but just as frequently he asks for help for *God's* own sake:

Let not those who hope in thee be put to shame through me,
O Lord God of hosts;
let not those who seek thee be brought to dishonor through me,
O God of Israel. —*Ps. 69:6*

Here the psalmist is concerned primarily with the glory of God, and only secondarily with his own salvation. If God does not intervene and save him, those who believe in God will be put to shame and God himself will be deprived of his glory. The psalmist's argument is strengthened by the fact that his predicament is in some way connected with his "zeal for [God's] house" (vs. 9), so that he feels he is suffering reproach and shame for God's sake (vs. 7). Thus the shame he has to bear affects God too, and the fact that God's glory is at stake is more important to him than his own troubles. At the same time, this verse exemplifies a feeling of fellowship, or social responsibility, as Leslie puts it. The misery of the psalmist tests the faith of other believers. They observe him and expect God to intervene and save him, and when help comes, this will also affect the whole congregation.

In a similar manner the national lament of Psalm 79 appeals to the glory of God's name:

> Help us, O God of our salvation,
> for the glory of thy name;
> deliver us, and forgive us our sins,
> for thy name's sake!
> Why should the nations say,
> "Where is their God?"
>
> —*Ps. 79:9,10*

Here the psalmist's concern is primarily that God's glory be restored and his righteousness revealed beyond all doubts. For if Israel suffers defeat, other nations will draw the conclusion that the God of Israel is weak and powerless, and God will not receive the glory that is due him. But if God does intervene, it is he and not Israel who is honored and glorified.

A similar prayer is found in Psalm 74, another national lament in which the psalmist deplores the desolation of the temple:[2]

> Remember this, O Lord, how the enemy scoffs,
> and an impious people reviles thy name.
> Do not deliver the soul of thy dove to the wild beasts;
> do not forget the life of thy poor for ever.
>
> —*Ps. 74:18,19*

Another pious Israelite, the author of Psalm 139, says about his enemies:

> Do I not hate them that hate thee, O Lord?
> And do I not loathe them that rise up against thee?
> I hate them with perfect hatred;
> I count them my enemies.   —*Ps. 139:21,22*

It is because they are God's enemies that they are also the enemies of the psalmist; he hates them, so to speak, "for God's sake." This is further accentuated, if the psalm, as several authors suggest, is in fact a renunciation of idolatry (cf. also Ps. 31:6). If we sense here a piety different from our own, it is because the concept of God involved may be somewhat different, and not because of any lack of a theocentric attitude.

The predominant interest in God's glory is well summarized in Psalm 115:

> Not to us, O Lord, not to us,
> but to thy name give glory,
> for the sake of thy steadfast love and thy faithfulness!
> Why should the nations say,
> "Where is their God?"
> Our God is in the heavens;
> he does whatever he pleases.   —*Ps. 115:1-3*

Here the setting is obviously the cult; the term "us" has reference to the congregation. The aim of the cult is not to increase the glory of the congregation, but to extol the glory of God. The concern of the congregation is that God's steadfast love and faithfulness should be revealed as effective realities in his activity in the world. The members of the community humbly bow before God and admit that they cannot themselves give God the glory due him. Only when God takes matters in his own hands and makes himself known in his deeds will he be properly glorified. The worshipers seem to say that they are not able to glorify God sufficiently, so they pray that God himself might glorify his name. For when God reveals his power and his faithfulness, even the heathen will acknowledge that he is God. We learn from this psalm something of the theocentric attitude prevalent in the cult. Indeed, the very source of the theocentric attitude in Israel is perhaps to be found in the cultic experience.[3]

There are in the Psalms several instances of curse formulas of an especially crude and primitive character, which in some cases still reveal traces of ancient ideas of sympathetic magic. Originally they may have been "effective spells," which were thought to work automatically. Once they were pronounced, their effect necessarily followed.[4] As an example we may cite some sentences from Psalm 58:

> O God, break the teeth in their mouths;
> tear out the fangs of the young lions, O Lord!
> Let them vanish like water that runs away;
> like grass let them be trodden down and wither.
> Let them be like the snail which dissolves into slime,
> like the untimely birth that never sees the sun.
> Sooner than your pots can feel the heat of thorns,
> whether green or ablaze, may he sweep them away!
>
> —*Ps. 58:6-9*

The curse formula has here been turned into a prayer—a prayer for vengeance, it is true, but nevertheless a prayer. Man no longer tries to achieve the punishment through magical manipulations, but the entire matter is placed in God's hands. Thus, again, the psalmist's ultimate concern is with God, even if his idea of God seems alien to us.[5]

The same is true, though to an even greater extent, in the case of the formulas of blessing. We know that a word of blessing was originally regarded as effective through its inherent power.[6] Once pronounced, the blessing was irrevocable; it worked irresistibly. In this way Jacob received the blessing of his father Isaac, and when the latter discovered that he had blessed the wrong person, he was not able to change what had occurred. Pedersen has described the *berakah* or "blessing" as the mysterious power, somewhat similar to the Melanesian *mana,* through which man is successful in all his doings. But Pedersen sometimes seems to forget a fact especially emphasized in the Psalms, namely, that for Israel all blessing comes from God.[7] In Psalm 127 we read:

> Unless the Lord builds the house,
> those who build it labor in vain.
> Unless the Lord watches over the city,
> the watchman stays awake in vain.
> It is in vain that you rise up early,
> to go late to rest,
> eating the bread of anxious toil;
> for he gives to his beloved in sleep.
>
> —*Ps. 127:1,2*

All effort is in vain, says the psalmist, if it is not accompanied by the Lord's blessing. For this reason there are many instances in the Psalms of prayers for this blessing from God. One example of such a prayer is:

> May God be gracious to us and bless us
> and make his face to shine upon us.
> . . . .
> God, our God, has blessed us.
> God has blessed us;
> let all the ends of the earth fear him!
> —*Ps. 67:1,6,7*

The first of the verses quoted appears to echo the benediction of Num. 6:24-26. It is thus another reminder of the importance of the cult in Israel, for this formula of blessing was supposed to be pronounced by the priests. Another formula, found in Ps. 118:26, "Blessed be he who enters in the name of the Lord," has been given the characteristic supplement: "We bless you from the house of the Lord." The blessing comes from the sanctuary, where the Lord is present. Similarly, there are two instances of the formula, "The Lord bless you from Zion!" (Pss. 128:5; 134:3), which expresses the same conviction: there is no blessing apart from God, but his presence in the temple means blessing to those who seek him there.

There is another instance of the theocentric attitude in the Psalms, although of a different character, in Psalm 30:

> As for me, I said in my prosperity,
> "I shall never be moved."
> By thy favor, O Lord,
> thou hadst established for me dignity and strength;[8]
> thou didst hide thy face,
> I was dismayed.   —*Ps. 30:6,7*

The prosperity of the psalmist made him secure; he trusted his own strength (cf. Ps. 10:6) and did not reckon with God as the Giver of all good things. In reality it was only through

God's favor that he possessed that which had filled him with such security. It was not until he encountered misfortune— "God hid his face"—that he realized that he had been mistaken.

It is emphasized several times in the Psalms that one can never rely on human resources, either on princes or on one's own strength (Pss. 118:6f.; 146:3). God is the only one who is able to help, and he has all power:

> On God rests my deliverance and my honor:
> my mighty rock, my refuge is God.
> Trust in him at all times, O people;
> pour out your heart before him;
> God is a refuge for us.
> Men of low estate[9] are but a breath,
> men of high estate[10] are a delusion;
> in the balances they go up;
> they are together lighter than a breath.
> —*Ps. 62:7-9*

In comparison with God, the secure refuge, all human resources are nothing but "a breath" and "a delusion," i.e., nothing to rely upon:

> A king is not saved by his great army;
> a warrior is not delivered by his great strength.
> The war horse is a vain hope for victory,
> and by its great might it cannot save.
> Behold, the eye of the Lord is on those who fear him,
> on those who hope in his steadfast love.—*Ps. 33:16-18*

As has already been indicated, it is foolishness to say that there is no God (Ps. 14:1) and to live accordingly, not seeking God and not calling upon him (Pss. 14:1,2b,4b; 53:2,3b,5). "In the pride of his countenance the wicked does not seek him; all his thoughts are, 'There is no God'" (Ps. 10:4). "God has forgotten, he will never see it" (Ps. 10:11). This is probably not theoretical atheism; the philosophical question of

God's existence is simply ignored, while people live and act as if God did not exist. This is what the Babylonians used to call "living *ina ramánishu*," i.e., living by oneself, on one's own resources, without dependence on God.[11] But this is the essence of sin; it will also be punished by God, when he "arises to plead his cause" (Ps. 74:22) and breaks the arm of the wicked (Ps. 10:12,15):

> But God will break you down for ever;
> he will snatch and tear you from your tent;
> he will uproot you from the land of the living.
> ....
> "See the man who would not make God his refuge,
> but trusted in the abundance of his riches,
> and sought refuge in his wealth!"   —*Ps. 52:5,7*

The fools in Psalm 14 will finally learn what they have done: "There they shall be in great terror, for God is with the generation of the righteous" (Ps. 14:5; cf. Ps. 53:5).

There are many gradations between the thoughtless security in days of prosperity and the open rebellion of the "wicked," but in both cases man tries to dethrone God—he does not let God be God, so to speak—and this is the very essence of sin.

Another essential aspect of sin is found in the well-known penitential psalm, Psalm 51:

> Against thee, thee only, have I sinned,
> and done that which is evil in thy sight,
> so that thou art justified in thy sentence
> and blameless in thy judgment. —*Ps. 51:4*

Here it is stated, first of all, that every sin is ultimately directed against God, because it expresses a fundamental attitude which does not care for God and will not let God be God. Secondly, it is implied that the goal of man's knowledge and confession of his sin has ultimately to do not with

35

man himself, but with God: it is to serve as a means of revealing *God's* righteousness, so that God is known and acknowledged as God (Weiser). This is theocentric piety.

Finally, another aspect of the theocentricity of the Psalms should be mentioned. There are in the Psalter some psalms that deal with the magnificence and beauty of creation and nature (Pss. 8, 19, 104). But nature is never praised for its own sake; there are no nature lyrics in the Psalms. Nature is referred to only to the extent that it points to him who made everything. Creation is not mentioned for its own sake, but for the Creator's sake. This again shows that it is God himself who is the focal point of the psalmist's interest.

CHAPTER 4

The Righteous and the Wicked

IN MANY of the psalms a sharp distinction is made between the righteous and the wicked. The first psalm describes the characteristics of these two kinds of people and dwells on the difference between their destinies. In other psalms a righteous sufferer cries out to God, complaining of assaults by the wicked. It is important that we find out what is really meant by this distinction. Who are the righteous, and who are the wicked? Is the distinction basically between those who are religious and those who are not, or are other factors involved?

In order to answer these questions we shall have to pay attention not only to the two terms "righteous" (*tsaddiq*) and "wicked" (*rasha*), but also to a number of synonymous and related words such as "godly," "saint," "poor," "needy," "oppressed," on one hand, and "sinners," "workers of evil," and the like, on the other. Unfortunately, a detailed investigation of each term based on the Hebrew text is not possible here. We shall have to confine ourselves to some remarks on a few of the terms in question.[1]

First there is the word *chasid*; translated as "saint" in the KJV, it usually appears in the RSV as "godly" or "faithful." In the Maccabean period this word was used to denote the "pious ones," who opposed every compromise with the religion of the Hellenistic rulers and who remained loyal to their inherited faith. At the time when most scholars thought the Psalms to have originated in the Maccabean period, the term was held to contain a reference to these "pious" Jews; but now, when most—if not all—of the psalms in question are believed to be pre-exilic, we must find a new interpretation of the word.

The word *chasid* occurs altogether twenty-one times in the Psalms. Unfortunately, not all the passages are clear, and some occurrences are not very illuminating. In Ps. 4:3 the context is somewhat obscure. In Ps. 12:1 we find that "godly" is more or less synonymous with "faithful"; elsewhere in this psalm the same people are referred to as "poor" or "needy" (vs. 5), and it is clear from the context that they are set in opposition to those who "utter lies" and "flatter" (vs. 2). In Ps. 16:10 the psalmist expresses the conviction that he, "the godly one," shall not have to "see the Pit" or be given up to Sheol—in other words, that he shall not die. But we learn nothing that could help us to define the word "godly." In Ps. 18:25 it is stated that God shows *chesed* ("loyalty") to those who are *chasid* ("loyal"). The point is obviously that God acts toward man according to man's own manner of living, which in this case must imply that the *chasid* is one who exercises *chesed,* "loyalty" or "steadfast love." The context also implies that "loyal" (*chasid*) falls into the same category as "blameless" and "pure" (see Ps. 18:25b,26); vs. 27 contains the expression "a humble people."

In Ps. 30:4 and Ps. 52:9 the "saints" or the "godly" are those who join in a psalm of thanksgiving or of lament; in other words, they play the role that is otherwise ascribed to the worshiping congregation. In the latter psalm we find that "the godly" are identical with "the righteous" (Ps. 52:6), and we note the opposition between the righteous who trust in God and his "steadfast love" (*chesed*), and the boasting "mighty man" of vs. 3 who trusts in himself and his wealth, i.e., who lives on his own apart from God—*ina ramânishu*, as the Babylonians say.

In Ps. 43:1 "an ungodly people" seems to be a merciless or deceitful people. In Ps. 89:19 the Hebrew text says: "Thou didst speak to thy faithful [or godly] ones," which seems to mean the congregation. The RSV, however, renders the expression in the singular number, making it refer to David.

In Ps. 86:2 "godly" is parallel to "servant," and vs. 14 shows that the psalmist's enemies are "insolent" and "ruthless." It has been argued that the use of the term "servant" indicates that the subject in this psalm is the king.[2] But even if this be true, there is nothing to show the exact meaning of the term "godly." Similarly, in Ps. 116:15, the context seems to indicate that "servant" and "godly" refer to the same person, but again we cannot be sure who is speaking and out of what situation. However, as in Psalm 16, there is reference to deliverance from "the snares of death" and "the pangs of Sheol" (Ps. 116:3; cf. vs. 8).

The remaining instances are somewhat different. In Ps. 50:5 it appears from the parallelism that "the faithful ones" are those who have made a covenant with God; in other words, they are Israel, God's people. In Ps. 79:2 "the saints" and "the servants" are obviously identical, and in this lament of the community it seems probable that the reference is to Israel as a people. But if so, it is apparent that the "saints" share in the sin that is confessed in the psalm and that they do not therefore form an especially pious group within the people. Similarly, Ps. 148:14 contains three expressions which seem more or less synonymous: "his people," "his saints," and "the people of Israel." Again in Psalm 149 "the assembly of the faithful" in vs. 1 refers to the same group as "the sons of Zion" and "Israel" in vs. 2, and probably also "his people" and "the humble" in vs. 4. It is likely that it is the whole people of Israel that is meant; "the assembly of the faithful" is the worshiping congregation of Israel, the people of the covenant, that participates in the *chesed* of the Lord, i.e., his "steadfast love" manifested in the covenant.[3]

Thus we find that the "saints" and "faithful" of the Psalms cannot be a religious sect or party, and that *chasid* is used synonymously or in parallelism with a number of other words: "humble," "oppressed," "needy," "blameless," "pure" "righteous," "servants," and "people."[4] But even if it is sometimes used with reference to the people as a whole, it obviously expresses some religious quality that the people have or should have. The etymology of the term and the context of Ps. 18:25 suggest that this quality is *chesed,* which originally means the pattern of behavior appropriate to those who share the fellowship of a covenant. In other words, the people of Israel, who are the object of God's "steadfast love" within the covenant, are expected to show this same love toward him and toward one another. This is another aspect of the attitude toward God expressed by the term "servant."

Besides the term *chasid* there are the two Hebrew words *ani* and *anaw,* which are generally translated as "oppressed" and "humble," respectively. It is obvious that the two words are closely related and that the difference in meaning is probably not so great as the English translation would seem to imply.[5] There are cases where "oppressed" is clearly equivalent to "poor" and "needy" and where "the oppressed" are really unjustly treated by others. But at the same time the word seems to have a religious connotation alluding to humility or lowliness before God. Possibly both shades of meaning could coexist.

In connection with *ani,* "oppressed," several words occur meaning "the poor" and "the needy" (afflicted). However, it is not certain as to whether these are poor in the literal sense or rather "poor in spirit." A study of all the passages in which the terms occur shows that there are a number of cases where the literal sense seems to fit the context, while there are other instances where either this is less probable or else it is difficult to determine what the exact meaning is. Using with some modifications a study by J. van der Ploeg,[6] we can make the following observations concerning the poor and needy in the Psalms:

1) They are generally described as being oppressed by the wicked. The causes of their misery are poverty or illness; sometimes persecution is also mentioned.

2) Passages where real poverty is probably referred to include Pss. 35:10; 41:1 (perhaps); 49:2; 82.3,4; 112:9; 113:7; 132:15.

3) The oppressed and poor cry to the Lord for help and protection in Pss. 25:16; 34:6; 40:17; 69:29; 70:5; 74:19,21; 86:1; 109:22. In these cases it is often difficult to determine whether there is a concrete situation of distress or if the psalmist is referring to his humble attitude before God.

4) In Ps. 37:14 the "poor and needy" are expressly equated with "those who walk uprightly" in contradistinction to "the wicked." In Ps. 18:27 ani, "humble," is contrasted with "haughty." Thus there are at least two definite instances where the "poor" or "afflicted" are supposed to have certain religious qualities.

5) In Ps. 34:2 and Ps. 69:32 the oppressed or afflicted function as the congregation, witnessing to God's intervention.

There is no reason to believe that the poor were known to be more righteous or more religious than the wealthy. On the contrary, there is a passage in Jer. 5:4 that indicates that the prophet expected the poor to be less religious than the other classes of society. In the Book of Proverbs we find a twofold attitude toward poverty. Normally poverty is the result of foolishness or wickedness, while wealth is the reward of wisdom and righteousness. On the other hand, righteousness is more valuable than wealth, and a poor man who is righteous is still a good man. In the Psalms most of the instances in which the poor are mentioned seem to refer to some concrete and specific situation of need. "Poor," "needy," and "oppressed" indicate this situation, but these expressions also indicate the ideal attitude of a man who is in need—humble acknowledgment of his dependence on God and submission to God's will. There may also be cases when these terms refer to the whole people in a situation of national distress and express the ideal attitude of submission to God, which in such a case should characterize the whole people.

It is noteworthy that even such an expression as "those who fear the Lord" occurs in contexts where it must refer to the whole people or the congregation, e.g.:

> He provides food for those who fear him;
> he is ever mindful of his covenant.
> He has shown his people the power of his works,
> in giving them the heritage of the nations.
> —*Ps. 111:5,6*

Since it was with the whole people that the Lord made his covenant, "those who fear him" should include all Israel.

Correspondingly, the "wicked" (*reshaim*) who appear in some laments of the community as the enemies of the righteous—i.e., of Israel—are obviously foreign, non-Israelitic nations (*goyim*) who are hostile to Yahweh and his people. This is the case, e.g., in Ps. 9:5:

> Thou hast rebuked the nations, thou hast destroyed the wicked;
> thou hast blotted out their name for ever and ever.

In vss. 15 and 16 of the same psalm there is again parallelism between "the nations," or "gentiles" (KJV), and "the wicked." In vs. 17 we find once more the same parallelism:

> The wicked shall depart to Sheol,
> all the nations that forget God.

In Ps. 10:16,17 "the nations" and "the meek" appear as opposites. In Ps. 50:7 ff. God addresses "his people" and in vss. 16 ff. "the wicked" are obviously the opposite of God's people.

A description of the wicked is given in Psalm 10:

> For the wicked boasts of the desires of his heart,
> and the man greedy for gain curses and renounces the Lord.[7]
> In the pride of his countenance the wicked does not seek him;
> all his thoughts are, "There is no God."
> His ways prosper at all times;
> thy judgments are on high, out of his sight;
> as for all his foes, he puffs at them.
> He thinks in his heart, "I shall not be moved;
> throughout all generations I shall not meet adversity."
> His mouth is filled with cursing and deceit and oppression;
> under his tongue are mischief and iniquity.
> . . . .
> He thinks in his heart, "God has forgotten,
> he has hidden his face, he will never see it." —Ps. 10:3-7,11

We see that the wicked one does not reckon with God or concern himself about God, but considers himself to be strong enough in his own power. In other words, he places himself outside God's domain, lives by himself, and does "not regard the works of the Lord, or the work of his hands" (Ps. 28:5).

It has been argued that in some cases in the Psalms the enemies are sorcerers and witches, and that especially the term "workers of evil" (*poale awen*) refers to such people.[8] There are, no doubt, many expressions in the Psalms that might be explained that way.[9] But it is remarkable that even the "workers of evil" sometimes direct their activity against the *people*:

> Have they no knowledge, all the evildoers
> who eat up my people as they eat bread,
> and do not call upon the Lord? —Ps. 14:4

Thus the enmity between righteous and wicked does not seem to exist between religious parties within the people itself, but between Israel as God's holy people or congregation, on one hand, and those who stand outside the covenant, on the other. Those standing outside the covenant could be national enemies; or they could be worshipers of foreign gods, or performers of magical practices forbidden by the Israelitic religion. There are scholars who deny the latter alternative and maintain that all enemies referred to in the Psalms are national or political enemies.[10] But we have seen that there are references in the Psalms to cases of broken religious fellowship, and if our understanding of such passages is correct, we must at least admit the possibility of religious dissension within the people, probably also occasioned by the existence of non-Yahwistic cult practices.

What has been said is not meant to deny that expressions like "godly," "humble," or "righteous" express desirable qualities. On the contrary, even when they are applied to the people or the congregation as a whole, they express a religious and ethical ideal that the people of God is to live up to, and to a certain extent does live up to, unlike those who stand outside of the cultic fellowship with Yahweh.

One fact remains to be noticed. There are some psalms in which the enemies of the psalmist are described as wild beasts, demons, or mythological monsters. One such psalm is Psalm 73:

> Therefore pride is their necklace;
> violence covers them as a garment.
> Their eyes swell out with fatness,
> their hearts overflow with follies.
> They scoff and speak with malice;
> loftily they threaten oppression.
> They set their mouths against the heavens,
> and their tongue struts through the earth.
> —Ps. 73:6-9

The last verse has an almost literal parallel in a text from the Ras Shamra tablets, which states that some mythological beings, who obviously have some connection with chaos and death, put one lip to the sky and the other to the earth and drain the water in abundance (cf. Ps. 73:10, especially the original Hebrew, which in the RSV is given in a footnote).[11]

Another case in point is Psalm 22:

> Many bulls encompass me,
> strong bulls of Bashan surround me;
> they open wide their mouths at me,
> like a ravening and roaring lion.
> . . . .
> Yea, dogs are round about me;
> a company of evildoers encircle me;
> they have pierced [?] my hands and feet.
> —*Ps. 22:12,13,16*

The psalmist's enemies are also God's enemies, and they are consequently regarded as being more or less identical with— or allies of—the forces of chaos. This is probably why they are described as wild beasts or monsters (cf. also Ps. 57:4). The imagery being mythological, the enemies are taken to be more than human; they become the representatives of all evil forces that threaten life and order in the world. That being so, we can understand why it may be a religious duty to hate the enemies: they threaten not only the individual or even the nation; they threaten the divine order of the world as it was established in the beginning. The enemies have placed themselves outside the sphere within which God is active and have joined the forces that work against him, trying to disturb or demolish the order that God established when he defeated the powers of chaos and created the world.

It has been suggested that the "enemy psalms" should be interpreted as rituals alluding to a symbolic drama, in which the attack upon and defeat of the evil forces was enacted.[12] Psalm 59 would be a case in point. Here the enemies are called "workers of evil" and "bloodthirsty men" (vs. 2), but also "howling dogs" (vss. 6,14)—which might be an allusion to demonic beings—and "nations" (gentiles, vss. 5,8), i.e., political enemies. All this can be taken as a way of summing up all the forces that are hostile to God, and the psalm would have its place in a cultic drama or sham fight, in which God's victory was represented—and to a certain extent accomplished —through symbolic actions.

We need only admit the possibility of such an interpretation. What is important for our study is the fact that the opposition between the righteous and their enemies—whether they are called "the wicked" or something else—is lifted up to a higher mythological or metaphysical level and related to the opposition between cosmos and chaos, or life and death, which, according to Pedersen, is so typical of the ancient Israelitic view of life.[13]

CHAPTER 5

The Concept of God

RELIGION IS man's response to his God. The shape and character of a religion, therefore, is determined by the believer's concept of God. The individual's personal experience of God and his concept of God are intimately related and mutually influence each other. Of the God of the Psalms it is said:

> ... power belongs to God;
> and to thee, O Lord, belongs steadfast love.
> —*Ps. 62:11,12*

In the combination of power and steadfast love the nature of the Old Testament belief in God is summarized. There is a "unity of opposites" in the Old Testament concept of God. Examples of this are easily found in many psalms. In Ps. 99:8 it is emphasized that God forgives the sins of his people, but requites their evil deeds:

> O Lord our God, thou didst answer them;
> thou wast a forgiving God to them,
> but an avenger of their wrongdoings.

In Ps. 68:35 the two aspects are tied together in the cultic experience:

> Terrible is God in his sanctuary,
> the God of Israel,
> he gives power and strength to his people.

The explanation of this statement is found in some earlier verses in the same psalm:

> Let God arise, let his enemies be scattered;
> let those who hate him flee before him!
> As smoke is driven away, so drive them away;
> as wax melts before fire,
> let the wicked perish before God!
> But let the righteous be joyful;
> let them exult before God;
> let them be jubilant with joy![1]
>
> . . . .
>
> O God, when thou didst go forth before thy people,
> when thou didst march through the wilderness,
> the earth quaked, the heavens poured down rain.
>
> . . . .
>
> Rain in abundance, O God, thou didst shed abroad;
> thou didst restore thy heritage as it languished;
> thy flock found a dwelling in it;
> in thy goodness, O God, thou didst provide for the needy.
>
> *—Ps. 68:1-3,7-10*

It is thus the cultic commemoration and actualization of God's mighty deeds in the past that forms the framework for the believer's experience of the terrible and good God. However, we can also discern a tendency apparent in many other psalms whereby God's goodness and mercy are held to be for the people of Israel, while his anger and wrath are intended for their enemies—who are, of course, also *his* enemies. But at the same time it must be remembered that the evaluation is always religious, made from the standpoint of God, not from that of the people or the nation as such.

To this twofold aspect of the concept of God there is a corresponding twofold attitude toward God on the part of the believer which might be expressed in Luther's words: "We should fear and love God." It is true that "fear of God" in the Old Testament has a more general meaning and usually does not mean more than "a religious attitude" or "piety" in general.² But nonetheless it is an established fact that the God of Israel is a terrible and dreadful God,

> who cuts off the spirit of princes,
> who is terrible to the kings of the earth.
> —*Ps. 76:12*

And it can be said of him:

> For we are consumed by thy anger;
> by thy wrath we are overwhelmed.
> . . . .
> Who considers the power of thy anger,
> and thy wrath according to the fear of thee?
> —*Ps. 90:7,11*

Here the nationalistic bias is absent, but it is clear that the human understanding does not easily grasp the full importance and dreadful consequences of the wrath of God. Such a God is to be feared. But it should not be forgotten that it is to the same God that the same psalmist prays: "Satisfy us . . . with thy steadfast love, that we may rejoice. . . . Make us glad. . . . Let the favor of the Lord our God be upon us" (Ps. 90:14,15,17).

The appropriate response to this terrible God is aptly expressed in the following verse:

> Let all the earth fear the Lord,
> let all the inhabitants of the world stand in awe of him!
> —*Ps. 33:8*

The verses which precede this in Psalm 33 mention God's power as revealed in the creation, and his victory over the powers of chaos, represented by "the ocean" or "the deep" (*tehom*). Thus the reference is to man's reaction before the mighty God who crushes all opposition and defeats all hostile powers, even the superhuman chaotic powers. Everything that stood in the way of the Creator's work was subdued by his mighty word. Should not man fear such a God? In what follows, the psalm also alludes to national enemies. Since they are God's enemies as well and threaten to upset the order he wants in his world, their defeat is of the same order as the defeat of the primeval powers of chaos. Nothing can stand against him; how could man do anything else but fear him?

The national and religious aspects merge in similar fashion also in Psalm 76:

> But thou, terrible art thou!
> Who can stand before thee
> when once thy anger is roused?
> From the heavens thou didst utter judgment;
> the earth feared and was still,
> when God arose to establish judgment
> to save all the oppressed of the earth.
>
> —*Ps. 76:7-9*

The help granted to God's people Israel, the "oppressed," reveals his terrible power, and the enemies are brought to silence: "the earth feared and was still."

Finally, a few verses from an enthronement psalm reveal another aspect of man's reaction when confronted with the greatness of his God:

> For great is the Lord, and greatly to be praised;
> he is to be feared above all gods.
> For all the gods of the peoples are idols;
> but the Lord made the heavens.
> Honor and majesty are before him;
> strength and beauty are in his sanctuary.
> Ascribe to the Lord, O families of the peoples,
> ascribe to the Lord glory and strength!
> Ascribe to the Lord the glory due his name;
> bring an offering, and come into his courts!
> Worship the Lord in holy array;
> tremble before him, all the earth!
>
> —*Ps. 96:4-9*

Here the Creator's presence in the sanctuary is featured. The reaction is humble and fearful adoration, expressed in the gesture alluded to by the Hebrew verb *hishtachawah,* "to prostrate oneself" with one's face to the ground, the deepest expression of reverence that was known at that time (cf. also Ps. 95:6). Thus it is recognized that all glory and power belong to the Lord, while all other "gods" are futile and powerless idols.[3]

The other aspect of the religious response, love for God, is rarely expressly mentioned in the Psalms. As a matter of fact, there is only one passage where it is clearly mentioned, namely, Ps. 18:1: "I love thee, O Lord, my strength."[4] In Ps. 116:1 ("I love the Lord, because he has heard my voice and my supplications") and Ps. 97:10 ("You who love the Lord hate evil," RSV marginal reading) the text is somewhat uncertain. To these references may be added some indirect evidence, namely, passages that speak of loving God's name (Pss. 5:11; 69:36)—the name is, so to speak, part of the person himself—or God's dwelling place (Ps. 26:8) or his law (several times in Psalm 119). In this group we can also include the well-known passage in Ps. 73:25: "there is nothing upon earth that I desire besides thee"; for here there is speaking a man to whom God means everything, a man who "even if his flesh and his heart may fail" has God as his strength and his portion (vs. 26). We might also mention Psalm 16 with its clear rejection of idol worship and its repeated protestations of the delight of being close to God:

> ... "I have no good apart from thee."
>
> . . . .
> The Lord is my chosen portion and my cup; ...
> The lines have fallen for me in pleasant places;
> yea, I have a goodly heritage.
>
> . . . .
> Thou dost show me the path of life;
> in thy presence there is fullness of joy,
> in thy right hand are pleasures for evermore.
>   —*Ps. 16:2,5,6,11*

Many details are obscure in this psalm, but there is no doubt that the one who is speaking rejoices that he has the Lord as his God and that he is trying to express something of the happiness of his fellowship with God.

But if the psalmists speak rarely of their love for God, all the more frequently do they refer to their longing for him, their waiting for his help, and their hope in him:

> As a hart longs
> for flowing streams,
> so longs my soul
> for thee, O God.
> *—Ps. 42:1*

> O God, thou art my God, I seek thee,
> my soul thirsts for thee;
> my flesh faints for thee,
> as in a dry and weary land where no water is.
> *—Ps. 63:1*

> "And now, Lord, for what do I wait?
> My hope is in thee."   *—Ps. 39:7*

> I wait for the Lord, my soul waits,
> and in his word I hope;
> my soul waits for the Lord
> more than watchmen for the morning,
> more than watchmen for the morning.
> *—Ps. 130:5,6*

These words are spoken in situations of distress or danger, but this does not lessen their religious value. It is interesting to study the words employed to express this attitude of longing and waiting. One is *qiwwah,* "to wait," from a root meaning originally "to stretch": the soul stretches out to reach God. Another is *yachal,* which combines the meanings "to hope" and "to wait." In times of distress and anxiety the soul stretches out toward God, knowing that in him there is hope for help and deliverance. The comparison with the thirsty traveler in the desert or the panting hart stretching out for life-giving water comes naturally to the mind of the psalmist.

It is worthy of notice, as regards the first two passages, that it is in the temple that the psalmist expects to satisfy his thirst.

There are also frequent references to the joy that the psalmists feel in contemplating God and his marvelous works:

> Then my soul shall rejoice in the Lord,
> exulting in his deliverance.   —*Ps. 35:9*

> For thou, O Lord, hast made me glad by thy work;
> at the works of thy hands I sing for joy.   —*Ps. 92:4*

> But may all who seek thee
> rejoice and be glad in thee;
> may those who love thy salvation
> say continually, "Great is the Lord!"
> —*Ps. 40:16*

> My lips will shout for joy,
> when I sing praises to thee;
> my soul also, which thou hast rescued.
> —*Ps. 71:23*

It would be easy to multiply examples, but even the few passages quoted convey a vivid impression of the joy and jubilation that characterize so many psalms. They also allow us to make two interesting observations. First, the joy of the psalmist is not due to the fact that God exists or that he has certain qualities. The reason for the psalmist's joy is that *God has done something*. Terms such as "his salvation," "his deeds," "the works of his hands," "his redemption," recur again and again. The God of the psalmist is an active God who intervenes for the benefit of his worshipers. Secondly, the joy of the psalmist is not a quiet feeling of happiness which he keeps to himself; rather the words employed are usually associated with praise of God in hymns or with the festive joy of the solemn celebrations in the temple. One may ask if the works of God referred to are not in many cases those actualized in the cult, such as the creation of the world and great events of the past. In other cases, of course, they represent things which have recently been experienced by the psalmist in his own life.

To this strain of joy must be added another: trust in God. This is the case, e.g., in the well-known shepherd's psalm (Psalm 23), in the words referring to God's rod and staff which comfort the psalmist even though he has to walk through the valley of deep darkness.[5] Sometimes this sense of security is defiantly expressed:

> In God I trust without a fear.
> What can man do to me?
> —*Ps. 56:11*[6]
> The Lord is my light and my salvation;
> whom shall I fear?
> The Lord is the stronghold of my life;
> of whom shall I be afraid?
> . . . .
> Though a host encamp against me,
> my heart shall not fear;
> though war arise against me,
> yet I will be confident.   —*Ps. 27:1,3*

Therefore we will not fear though the earth should change, though the mountains shake in the heart of the sea.
> —*Ps. 46:2*

That is, even if the very order of the world were overthrown, the believer would be secure in God.

In other cases the confidence expressed is more meditative and quiet:

> For God alone my soul waits in silence;
> from him comes my salvation.
> He only is my rock[7] and my salvation,
> my fortress; I shall not be greatly moved.
> —*Ps. 62:1,2; cf. vs. 6*

He who dwells in the shelter of the Most High,
who abides in the shadow of the Almighty,
will say to the Lord, "My refuge and my fortress;
my God, in whom I trust."

. . . .

> he will cover you with his pinions,
> and under his wings you will find refuge;
> his faithfulness is a shield and buckler.
> —*Ps. 91:1,2,4*

The last-mentioned psalm continues making reference to safety from illness, demons, and all kinds of danger:

> A thousand may fall at your side,
> ten thousand at your right hand;
> but it will not come near you.
> —*Ps. 91:7*

The psalmist feels safe, whatever happens to him, knowing that he is under God's protection. Trusting in God, he is patiently at rest and his anxiety is removed, for he knows that God grants "salvation," i.e., deliverance, freedom, and the possibility of living a rich and full life. Under God's protection he is safe as the young bird under the wings of its mother,[8] or as the soldier of that time was behind his stout shield.

Thus the pious man knows that God is with him. Wherever he goes, God's eye always beholds him. This means comfort and security, but also a vivid awareness of the impossibility of escaping God's searching scrutiny:

> Whither shall I go from thy Spirit?
> Or whither shall I flee from thy presence?
> If I ascend to heaven, thou art there!
> If I make my bed in Sheol, thou art there! '
> If I take the wings of the morning
> and dwell in the uttermost parts of the sea,
> even there thy hand shall lead[9] me,
> and thy right hand shall hold me.
> —*Ps. 139:7-10*

We could hardly find a better expression for God's omnipresence. Wherever in the universe a man might be, he is encompassed by God's presence. And what are the implications of

God's omnipresence for the pious individual? The same psalm
gives the answer a few lines farther down:

> Search me, O God, and know my heart!
> Try me and know my thoughts!
> And see if there be any wicked way in me,
> and lead me in the way everlasting!
> —*Ps. 139:23,24*[10]

It is impossible to deceive the All-knowing and All-seeing
One. It is necessary, therefore, to live openly and sincerely
before him. This implies both responsibility and assistance.
No one can escape responsibility for his life and his works.
But, on the other hand, if one is willing to accept God's omnipresence, one can trust God and expect him to lead and guide
in the right way. This basic attitude remains the same, if—as
is very probable—the "wicked way" is in reality "a way of
idols," i.e., idol worship.

It has recently been argued by a Dutch scholar, H. J.
Franken, that there are traces of a sense of "mystical communion" with God in the Psalms."[11] This is surprising, since
it is otherwise generally agreed that there is no mysticism to
be found in the Old Testament. The term "mysticism," however, can be used with several meanings. If it is taken to denote "the experience of union or identification with the
deity," as is often the case, there is certainly no mysticism in
the Psalms. But if it is employed in the sense of "intimate and
immediate communion with God," there are some expressions
in the Psalms that should at least be discussed in this connection.

First, there is a word that is rendered by the RSV as "to
meditate" (*siach*), but is taken by Franken as an expression
for man's being so filled with the divine that we can speak of
a mystic experience.

There are three passages especially that should be considered:

Of the glorious splendor of thy majesty,
and of thy wondrous works, I will meditate.
—Ps. 145:5

I will meditate on all thy work,
and muse on thy mighty deeds.
—Ps. 77:12

I remember the days of old,
I meditate on all that thou hast done;
I muse on what thy hands have wrought.
—Ps. 143:5

Here we can make these observations: (1) The object of the verb is not God, but his works. (2) In the first passage the expression occurs in a context in which words such as "proclaim," "declare," and "praise" are predominant. Accordingly, there is not only silent meditation, but an audible proclamation of the insight that has been attained.[12] (3) In the last two passages *siach* is used together with *hagah*, which actually does not mean to "muse" (RSV) but to mutter religious phrases, so that "the individual loses himself in his religion," as Franken with some exaggeration has put it.[13] (4) In the last passage we find also the verb *zakar*, "to remember," which in Hebrew thought means "the actualization of something to the degree that it fills the soul of the individual and determines his actions." (5) Finally this same passage is immediately followed by an expression of the soul's longing and thirst for God, which, to judge from the context, implies longing for his help in distress. In summary, it seems apparent that it is God's mighty deeds that fill the soul and occupy it to the extent that the result is either praise or confident longing for a new divine intervention. But there is no quiet meditation, nor any mystical identification with God.

We have already quoted a passage referring to "being silent" before God. This was Ps. 62:1, where we found an expression of the security felt under God's protection. A similar expression is found in Ps. 37:7:

> Be still before the Lord, and wait patiently for him;
> fret not yourself over him who prospers in his way.

It emerges clearly from the context that the reference is to waiting patiently for God's help without trying to take the matter into one's own hands. Psalm 37:9 again speaks of those who wait for the Lord, and promises them ultimate success. There is no mystical meditation or absorption in the divine, but confidence and trust in God. The psalmist's conviction of God's ultimate, final intervention is so firm that he dares to wait.

We may come closer to the mystical relationship with God in two other expressions which we find in the following passages:

> My soul clings to thee;
> thy right hand upholds me.
> —*Ps. 63:8*

> Because he cleaves to me in love, I will deliver him;
> I will protect him, because he knows my name.
> —*Ps. 91:14*

In the first passage the Hebrew uses the verb *dabaq*, which means that two different elements cleave together without actually becoming one.[14] The tongue "cleaves" to the jaw (Ps. 22:15); the waistcoat "clings" to the loins of a man (Jer. 13:11); a man "cleaves" to his wife (Gen. 2:24). Applied to man's relationship to God, this indicates intimate fellowship, perhaps love, but not absorption in God. This is still clearer in the original text, which uses the preposition "after," thus literally "to cleave after," i.e., to follow closely after God. In the second passage the verb is *chashaq*. The original meaning of this verb seems to be "being joined with or attached to somebody"; it is used especially with reference to conjugal love. The context alludes to protection and deliverance, but also to the knowing of God's name, which is also an expression of intimate fellowship.[15]

58

In Ps. 25:14 there is another interesting expression: "The friendship of the Lord is for those who fear him." The word *sod,* which is employed here, means "confidential conversation and intimate relationship" (Bentzen) or "an intimate personal relationship," in which "the pious are in perfect peace with God and entirely in [accord] with his will" (Franken).[16] It is, of course, easy to overemphasize the importance of such a passage and read too much into it, but we clearly sense here something of the intimacy suggested in Amos 3:7: The Lord reveals his *sod* (RSV: "secret") to the prophets. The passage quoted from Psalm 25 might refer to a revelation of God's will to man, so that the believer will not transgress against it. It is to be noted that we are dealing with an aspect of the covenant relationship between God and his people.

Several times the psalmists employ the word "good" in connection with man's relationship with God. "O taste and see that the Lord is good! Happy is the man who takes refuge in him" (Ps. 34:8). God's goodness is often combined with his steadfast love (e.g., Ps. 106:1) or with his help, which is probably also the case in Psalm 34 (see vss. 4,6). In Ps. 73:28 the psalmist asserts that "it is good to be near God" (or, perhaps, "to draw near God," i.e., in the temple worship). But it is rather difficult to determine the emotional reality that is behind the expression "good" in these and similar statements. The Hebrew word *tob* has at least as many shades of meaning as its English equivalent.

To these examples, all of which are also discussed by Franken, we might add two more. In Ps. 31:5 we read: "Into thy hand I commit my spirit," i.e., "entrust it to thy care," an expression of confidence and security, which is further emphasized through the references in the context to deliverance and redemption. Finally, we want once more to call attention to Psalm 16, in which such words as "good," "pleasant," and "goodly" convey the impression of emotional involvement. We should also notice the combination of security and joy in Ps. 16:9: "My heart is glad, and my soul rejoices; my body dwells secure." Body and soul—i.e., the whole man—is engaged in the experience of the divine goodness.

In none of these cases do we find anything that goes beyond communion or fellowship with God; there is no *unio mystica* or identification with the deity. God remains God, and man remains man. Man can experience God's nearness and goodness in joy and gratitude; he can be lifted up and sustained by the cultic experience; he can tremble before the Holy and Terrible One. But he is not absorbed by the mystic experience so as to become united with God.

A French scholar, André Neher, has defined man's love for God in the Old Testament as "conjugal love" and added the remark: "Mystic love is love *in* God. The conjugal love of the Old Testament is love *with* God."[17] This is a correct observation. The Old Testament man "walks with God" in fear and love, but he is never mystically absorbed by the deity. The distinction and distance between God and man remain in spite of the most intimate fellowship.

CHAPTER 6

Lament and Confession

WE MIGHT expect that in order to know the people behind the Psalms it would be appropriate to turn primarily to the psalms of lament; such psalms presumably reflect situations in which a person is likely to disclose his feelings without inhibition. But this expectation is fulfilled only to a very limited extent. As has already been emphasized, these psalms give little or no information concerning the individual destiny of the suppliant, nor do they tell much about the details of his suffering. On the contrary, it may even be said with some justification that the psalms of lament are more stereotyped than any other group, especially where a description of suffering is concerned. Familiar images are chosen, stereotyped phrases used, and everything shaped by the traditional style of the lament. Consequently, it is very difficult to determine what kind of suffering is actually being referred to, nor does it become easier when in the same psalm the suppliant complains of both illness and enemies, as happens in a number of cases (Pss. 38:5, 7, 12, 19; 41:2, 3; 102:5, 8).

Why is the individual pushed into the background in such a way that only general features appear? There is an interesting remark in this connection in Franken's book *The Mystical Communion*.[1] Franken says that when a man is threatened

61

by danger, when a calamity befalls him, he feels confused as long as he does not recognize the nature of his misfortune. As long as one does not understand a changing situation, nor succeed in defining a new situation, one is entirely lost. If the normal order of things breaks down and chaos threatens life, the first thing to be done is to make use of a religious pattern to change the unknown danger into a well-known danger. This way of defining what happens outside the normal order of things is designed to prevent bewilderment from taking possession of the mind and paralyzing the will.[2] Thus, according to Franken, the need to recognize a situation and the traditional points of view themselves work together to give the pattern a creative function. One recognizes a situation by imposing a relevant pattern on it and at the same time shaping the situation to make it conformable to the pattern.[3] There is, consequently, a lack of concrete details in the description of the psalmist's need. As a matter of fact, there is no actual description of the situation; it is only classified according to the interpretation suggested by the pattern. There is thus movement in two directions: the event calls to the mind its corresponding pattern and the pattern shapes the event in its characteristic form.[4]

As we shall presently see, the suffering of the suppliant in the psalms of lament is often expressed in such a way as to suggest that he is in the power of Sheol, or the realm of death. According to Franken, the superhuman, nondivine world is endowed with the characteristics of Sheol. This is the common pattern that comes to mind for people in deep distress. Here we clearly see how the pattern influences the mind and causes it to see characteristic features of the pattern in a situation of danger. It is the realm of death which reaches up to extend its authority and power over the life of the sufferer. In most cases no attention is paid to those features by which the situation would be described from our occidental point of

view. The idea of broken unity or harmony is wholly dominant and overshadows the real causes.[5]

This should be borne in mind when we proceed to survey
briefly some psalms of lament in order to see how in these
psalms suffering and need is conceived. We must not expect
to find details concerning the misfortune of particular individuals. Rather we shall find a general interpretation of suffering as such.

In spite of the stereotyped pattern to be found in these
psalms, the description of suffering is often very vivid and
does not at all lack poetical power, as is evident in the following verses:

> I am poured out like water,
> and all my bones are out of joint;
> my heart is like wax,
> it is melted within my breast;
> my strength is dried up like a potsherd,
> and my tongue cleaves to my jaws;
> thou dost lay me in the dust of death.
> ....
> I can count all my bones.
>   —Ps. 22:14,15,17

We do not know if illness is being described in these lines,
for the psalm also refers to enemies. But it is clear that the
psalmist feels abandoned to all evil powers, even to death.
Illness is potential death. There is no essential difference between illness and death, but only a difference in degree, since
in both cases the same powers are at work.

But other kinds of suffering too may be described, using
the same pattern:

> For my soul is full of troubles,
> and my life draws near to Sheol.
> I am reckoned among those who go down to the Pit;
> I am a man who has no strength,
> like one forsaken among the dead,

> like the slain that lie in the grave,
> like those whom thou dost remember no more,
> for they are cut off from thy hand.
> Thou hast put me in the depths of the Pit,
> in the regions dark and deep.
> Thy wrath lies heavy upon me,
> and thou dost overwhelm me with all thy waves.
> —*Ps. 88:3-7*

There is a great variety of opinion as to the character of the suffering reflected in this psalm, whether it is illness, imprisonment (cf. "shut in," vs. 8), or the ritual suffering of the king in the New Year's festival.[6] From our point of view it is more important to observe that the suppliant feels that he is in the power of death, or in Sheol, the realm of the dead. He is cut off from God's hand, i.e., from divine help, and feels as if he were outside the sphere of God's authority and power. The world of death is trying to infringe upon the realm of life. The forces that are hostile to God seem to have won a victory. But in spite of all this, God is not entirely excluded, for it is his wrath that has caused the suppliant's misery (vs. 8).

> The cords of death[7] encompassed me,
> the torrents of perdition assailed me;
> the cords of Sheol entangled me,
> the snares of death confronted me.
> —*Ps. 18:4,5*

The "cords" and the "snares" are easily understood poetic images. But why the reference to "torrents"? Consideration of the ancient conception of the world will provide the answer. If we imagine that Sheol is situated somewhere beneath the earth and that the earth is a flat disk, floating in the ocean, we understand why the psalmists so often speak of water, streams, and waves in connection with the realm of death. The same imagery is common in Babylonian psalms.[8] Here is another example:

> Save me, O God!
> For the waters have come up to my neck.
> I sink in deep mire,
> where there is no foothold;
> I have come into deep waters,
> and the flood sweeps over me.
> *—Ps. 69:1,2*

In his desperate plight the psalmist cries out to his God:

> I am weary with my crying;
> my throat is parched.
> My eyes grow dim
> with waiting for my God.
> *—Ps. 69:3*

A similar condition seems to be indicated in Psalm 42:

> As a hart longs
> for flowing streams,
> so longs my soul
> for thee, O God.
> My soul thirsts for God,
> for the living God.
> . . . .
> Deep calls to deep
> at the thunder of thy cataracts;
> all thy waves and thy billows
> have gone over me.
> *—Ps. 42:1,2,7*

It is almost certainly erroneous to understand the waves and the cataracts as allusions to the geography of northern Palestine, where the psalmist lives in exile. The waters must have a symbolic meaning. They are images referring to the realm of death: the psalmist is in the power of death and Sheol. Incidentally, it is remarkable that a man dwelling among waters should express his longing for God in the image of thirst. This is another proof of the stereotyped character of the language of the Psalms: even two incompatible images may be combined.

In the sequel there is reference to mocking enemies:

> As with a deadly wound in my body,
> my adversaries taunt me,
> while they say to me continually,
> "Where is your God?"   —*Ps. 42:10*

In this last verse we touch upon one of the greatest problems of the psalms of lament: the feeling of being abandoned by God. It is not enough that the sufferer is abandoned by men, that the fellowship in worship is broken, and that his friends have become his enemies, mocking him. He feels as if God too had left him, and finally he breaks out in despair: "Why hast thou forgotten me?" (Ps. 42:9).

We find the same problem in Psalm 22, a psalm in which faith and doubt struggle from the first line to the last:

> My God, my God, why hast thou forsaken me?
> Why art thou so far from helping me,
>   from the words of my groaning?
> O my God, I cry by day, but thou dost not answer;
> and by night, but find no rest.   —*Ps. 22:1,2*

The psalmist is surrounded by enemies and despised by his fellow men:

> But I am a worm, and no man;
> scorned by men, and despised by the people.[9]
> All who see me mock at me,
> they make mouths at me, they wag their heads.
>   —*Ps. 22:6,7*

It is hard to determine what sort of suffering is referred to in this psalm, in which both illness and attacks of enemies are mentioned. But to understand the mockery and the contempt it is helpful to remember that, according to the Old Testament, suffering and illness and sin are closely related. He who sins is punished by suffering, and he who suffers must have sinned. A sinner is not worthy of fellowship with other members of the community. Consequently, the sufferer is aban-

doned by his friends and his fellow worshipers. It even seems
to him that they have become his enemies. Bearing in mind
what we have learned about the importance of fellowship to
the Old Testament man, we easily realize what it meant for a
suffering man to be cut off from his normal relationship with
other people. Such ostracism added tremendously to his suffering: he had to bear his bodily pain alone, he had to be without his friends, he felt abandoned by God—and, in addition
to this, he knew that his suffering must be the result of God's
wrath.

The connection between sin and suffering is often expressly
stated,[10] e.g.:

> There is no soundness in my flesh
> because of thy indignation;
> there is no health in my bones
> because of my sin.
> For my iniquities have gone over my head;
> they weigh like a burden too heavy for me.
> My wounds grow foul and fester
> because of my foolishness,
> I am utterly bowed down and prostrate;
> all the day I go about mourning.
>
> —*Ps. 38:3-6*

Thus the psalmist's illness is the consequence of sin; it is
God's punishment for the "foolishness" of sin. Clearly his
friends will have no intercourse with a man punished by God:

> My friends and companions stand aloof from my plague,
> and my kinsmen stand afar off. —*Ps. 38:11*

The suffering of the psalmist is both psychic and physical:

> For my loins are filled with burning,
> and there is no soundness in my flesh.
> . . . .
> My heart throbs, my strength fails me;
> and the light of my eyes—it also has gone from me.
>
> —*Ps. 38:7,10*

From a psychological point of view this is easy to understand. Modern medicine knows that physical and mental suffering are closely related and mutually influence each other. But the Israelitic conception of man, according to which body and soul constitute a totality, also provides for such psychosomatic understanding. Physical suffering isolates man and deprives him of the possibility of a normal life in communion with the congregation of God, and isolation causes psychic suffering which is increased by the sufferer's consciousness of carrying a burden of sin.

Suffering therefore opens the eyes of the poor man; he realizes his guilt and confesses his sin:

> I confess my iniquity,
> I am sorry for my sin.
> —*Ps. 38:18*

Confession of sin holds an important place in the psalms of lament, some of which may even be called psalms of confession or penitentials. Psalm 51 is too well known to be quoted in full; we select only a few verses:

> Have mercy on me, O God, according to thy steadfast love;
> according to thy abundant mercy blot out my transgressions.
> Wash me thoroughly from my iniquity,
> and cleanse me from my sin! —*Ps. 51:1,2*

Here there seems to be an allusion to some rite of washing to symbolize purification from sin.

> For I know my transgressions,
> and my sin is ever before me.
> Against thee, thee only, have I sinned,
> and done that which is evil in thy sight.
> . . . .
> Behold, I was brought forth in iniquity,
> and in sin did my mother conceive me.
> —*Ps. 51:3-5*

There is probably no doctrine of original sin in the last verse, but rather a strong expression—perhaps poetically exaggerated[11]—of the psalmist's feeling of being entirely and totally sinful.

He goes on to say:

> Purge me with hyssop, and I shall be clean;
> wash me, and I shall be whiter than snow.
> —*Ps. 51:7*

Here again there seems to be an allusion to some rite of purification. It may be that these expressions should be understood in a figurative sense, although it is hard to see how they could have originated if some such ceremonies had not at one time existed. But if we grant that such rites did occur in Israel, we should not immediately depreciate them as mere externalism. The deep insight into the essence and nature of sin which is found in this psalm could obviously exist alongside outward rites which served as visible signs of the forgiveness of sins, namely, washing, hyssop, and the wiping out of sins written on a tablet. Such a rite is known in Babylonia. The existence of outward signs does not necessarily make the religious experience less "spiritual"; it only serves to reinforce the experience. Religion occupies the whole man, and the religious life is accordingly influenced by sense impressions called forth by symbolic actions.

In Psalm 51 we do not hear much of suffering, though an allusion to it may perhaps be found in vs. 8:

> Make me hear[12] joy and gladness;
> let the bones which thou hast broken rejoice.

But this might also be figurative speech. Furthermore, the joy that the psalmist wants to hear could be some kind of absolution spoken by a priest.

Another psalmist tells how he tried to escape the humiliating acknowledgment of his sinfulness and was unwilling to confess his sin until he experienced something that forced him to speak:

> When I declared not my sin, my body wasted away
> through my groaning all day long.
> For day and night thy hand was heavy upon me;
> my strength was dried up as by the heat of summer.
> I acknowledged my sin to thee,
> and I did not hide my iniquity;
> I said, "I will confess my transgressions to the Lord";
> then thou didst forgive the guilt of my sin.
>
> *—Ps. 32:3-5*

We shall never know whether the psalmist refers to physical pain which finally became so intense that he could stand it no longer, or whether he describes pangs of conscience which finally caused him so much anguish that he could not be silent. The latter alternative would be quite possible and even probable from a psychological point of view. But in view of the close relationship between bodily and mental suffering in the Psalms it is impossible to reach certainty at this point.

In Babylonian psalms of lament the fact that a man has suffered misfortune is frequently taken to mean that he must have sinned in some way even without knowing it,[13] so that it is necessary to find out what his sin is. Accordingly, it is not unusual that forgiveness is asked for sins which are unknown to the speaker. This presupposes a rather mechanical conception of sin: if man has transgressed some of the precepts of the gods, whether he is aware of his transgression or not, punishment will necessarily come.

There are very few traces of such a conception in the Psalms. The only evident example is Ps. 19:12: "But who can discern his errors? Clear thou me from hidden [faults]." The reference is obviously to unintentional sins committed unknowingly, and therefore "hidden" even to the sinner himself. For such sins the psalmist asks God's forgiveness—or rather, acquittal or exoneration. Probably the *alumim* or

70

"hidden things" in Ps. 90:8 (RSV: "secret sins") are also such sins. But even if it is clear from the context that the word refers to sins, these sins need not necessarily be unconscious or unintentional. They could also be sins hidden or kept secret from others, thus an instance of hypocrisy.[14]

The Israelite psalmists have, for the most part, a more personal conception of sin: they know their errors, they are aware that they have sinned against God, but they also know that the only way out is to return to God through penitence and confession:

> But there is forgiveness with thee,
> that thou mayest be feared.
> —*Ps. 130:4*

The same personal concept of sin is behind the protestations of innocence that we find in such psalms as Pss. 7, 17, 26, 59:

> If thou triest my heart, if thou visitest me by night,
> if thou testest me, thou wilt find no wickedness in me;
> my mouth does not transgress.
> . . . .
> My steps have held fast to thy paths,
> my feet have not slipped.   —*Ps. 17:3,5*

> Vindicate me, O Lord,
> for I have walked in my integrity.
> . . . .
> Prove me, O Lord, and try me;
> test my heart and my mind.
> For thy steadfast love is before my eyes,
> and I walk in faithfulness to thee.
> I do not sit with false men,
> nor do I consort with dissemblers.
> —*Ps. 26:1-4*

Generally these declarations of innocence are connected with complaints about the violent deeds of the psalmist's enemies;

he protests that they hate him without cause or reason, for he knows that he is innocent. That he should have sinned unconsciously is out of the question. (If these psalms, as is assumed by many scholars,[15] are prayers of persons falsely accused of some crime, the situation would be somewhat changed. In that case the protestation of innocence would concern only the crime actually in question. But these protestations often have such a universal and categorical form that this interpretation is not very probable).

If, according to the Old Testament, sin and suffering are inseparable, the success and prosperity of the wicked pose a problem with which the pious must struggle. Thus in Psalm 73 the psalmist is vexed by the prosperity of the wicked. He describes their rampaging in terms of mythological figures, equating them with evil, chaotic powers.[16] He cannot understand why God permits this while he himself—despite his innocence—is tormented:

> But when I thought how to understand this,
> it seemed to me a wearisome task,
> until I went into the sanctuary of God;
> then I perceived their end.
> Truly thou dost set them in slippery places;
> thou dost make them fall to ruin.
> How they are destroyed in a moment,
> swept away utterly by terrors! —*Ps. 73:16-19*

In the temple the psalmist learned of the destiny in store for those who oppose God and revolt against him. They will share the fate of all the evil powers defeated by Yahweh. The reference may be to the symbolic representation of God's triumph over the powers of chaos in creation, as dramatized in the New Year's festival. But the reference may also be to dramatizations of the historical tradition of the deliverance from Egypt. The experience, through the cult, of the present reality of these redemptive acts gives the psalmist the solution to his problem, and he says:

Nevertheless I am continually with thee;
thou dost hold my right hand.
Thou dost guide me with thy counsel,
and afterward thou wilt receive me to [?] glory.
Whom have I in heaven [but thee]?
And there is nothing upon earth that I desire besides thee.
My flesh and my heart may fail,
but God is the strength of my heart and my portion for ever.
—*Ps. 73:23-26*

The certainty of God's final victory gives the psalmist courage to remain with his God in spite of everything, and in communion with God the psalmist finds all that he desires upon this earth: "for me it is good to be near God" (Ps. 73:28).[17]

We have seen that in the psalms of lament the suppliant is often described as going down to Sheol, or as sinking into mire and waters. Therefore salvation can be described in corresponding figures of speech:

I waited patiently for the Lord;
he inclined to me and heard my cry.
He drew me up from the desolate pit,
out of the miry bog,
and set my feet upon a rock,
making my steps secure.
—*Ps. 40:1,2*

The "desolate pit" is the nether world, Sheol; the "miry bog" is in itself a telling figure for the sufferer's sense of helplessness and despair—he feels as if he were sinking into a bottomless abyss—but it is also related to the common imagery of water and ocean depths. The firm foothold on the rock forms an impressive contrast, depicting deliverance from death and the security that is experienced under the protection of God.

Sometimes deliverance from death is described in more forthright terms:

> For thou hast delivered my soul from death,
> my eyes from tears,
> my feet from stumbling;
> I walk before the Lord
> in the land of the living. —*Ps. 116:8,9*

> I shall not die, but I shall live,
> and recount the deeds of the Lord.
> The Lord has chastened me sorely,
> but he has not given me over to death.
> —*Ps. 118:17,18*

Of course, the fact that salvation is described as escape from death tells us nothing about the nature of the danger, since almost any suffering or calamity can be described as caused by the powers of death or Sheol. It is even possible that the two psalms just quoted refer to a symbolic representation of the attack and defeat of the evil powers at the New Year's festival—in that case, the subject of the psalms would be the king as the representative of his people—but the essential thing for us is the conviction that it is God who has the upper hand. God is able to conquer all the evil powers which try to work death and destruction on earth. He is stronger than death and chaos, and his power is not limited by death. Life and death are in his hand, and he is able to give life to those who are threatened by death:

> For thou dost not give me up to Sheol,
> or let thy godly one see the Pit.
> —*Ps. 16:10*

> But God will ransom my soul from the power of Sheol,
> for he will receive me. —*Ps. 49:15*

It is never stated *how* this deliverance takes place; it is enough to know *that* God will not deliver the psalmist's soul up to death and Sheol. Nowhere, however, in the Psalms is there a reference to resurrection or eternal life. The psalmists are content to know that God is stronger than death and

Sheol. It may be that they have had in mind God's triumph in creation over the powers of chaos and death, or an actual deliverance from some specific illness or calamity. But this is never expressly stated. They speak in terms of death and life, without spelling out their beliefs concerning the destiny of the individual soul after death, except for some general statements about Sheol, where nobody can praise the Lord (Pss. 6:5, 88:10,11). But their faith that God is stronger than death provides the presupposition for an added assurance: that God does not leave the pious man in death but is with him also beyond death.

CHAPTER 7

Thanksgiving and Praise

It is a remarkable fact that many psalms of lament (e.g., Pss. 22 and 28) end with thanksgiving. This is hard to explain. Even if it is psychologically true that the assurance of being heard often comes while one is praying, it is doubtful whether this inward assurance is sufficient to explain the thanksgiving for actual help that we find in these psalms. A theory which has much in its favor suggests that after the recitation of a lament or a confession in the temple a priest or prophet would proclaim God's favorable acceptance of the prayer and the promise of his help. The thanksgiving would then be the psalmist's response to this "absolution." A divine answer to a psalm, although of a somewhat different character, is to be found in Ps. 91:14 ff.[1] We must assume that it was proclaimed by a divine representative or spokesman belonging to the class of priests or prophets.

But even if we assume that a divine answer causes the sudden shift of mood in these psalms, the thanksgiving would still be for things unseen. Such thanksgiving would be an act of faith, for the deliverance would not yet be a reality. The psalmist would be thanking God out of reliance upon the truth of the divine proclamation.

Quite apart from these psalms of lament, however, thanksgiving and praise constitute one of the dominant themes in the Psalms generally. It is characteristic of true piety that it not only turns to God in times of distress, but also remembers to thank him in times of success and prosperity. Therefore thanksgiving is highly prized in the Psalms; in a few cases it is even equated with an acceptable sacrifice (Pss. 50:14; 69:30 f.).[2]

We often distinguish between thanksgiving and praise. One thanks God for a specific gift or for deliverance from a certain danger or calamity, but one praises him for his greatness, goodness, and power, and for his mighty deeds. Thanksgiving is the affair of an individual, while praise belongs to the worshiping congregation and has its proper place at the great festivals in the hymns extolling the Creator, King, and Redeemer. It is also thought that praise is more spontaneous and free, while thanksgiving is a duty. Or it is suggested that in thanksgiving the individual and his interests are emphasized, while in praise attention is directed to God alone.[3]

It must be said, however, that this is a modern distinction not found in the Psalms or in the Old Testament generally. Even a casual study of the Hebrew words for "thanksgiving" and "to thank" (*todah* and *hodah*) will show that this is so. The root from which the verb is formed means "to acknowledge," "to admit," and "to confess." Consequently, thanksgiving is not primarily an expression of gratitude to God, but rather the admission or acknowledgment that it is God who has acted and that the psalmist is entirely dependent on him. Thanksgiving is a confession and a proclamation of God as the one from whom all good gifts come. Thus thanksgiving is no less theocentric than the praise of God's greatness.[4] It is inaccurate to distinguish between them on the grounds that thanksgiving is more man-centered, while praise is purely God-centered.[5]

From the way the word "to thank" is often closely connected with such expressions as "to praise" or "to bless" God, it is evident that no real distinction between the two concepts is intended (e.g., Pss. 100:4; 109:30). Thanksgiving is the proper response to God's actions, but it expresses itself in praise.[6] Thanksgiving is simply one way of praising God, and it is characteristic that the Greek translation of the Old Testament usually renders *todah* as *ainesis,* i.e., "praise."[7]

Some modern scholars distinguish between descriptive praise, which refers quite generally to God and his greatness, and narrative praise, which celebrates some specific events. Much can be said in favor of this distinction.[8] While a detailed study of the various words for "praise" that are used in the Psalms is not possible here, it should be noted that roughly speaking they can be classified in two groups. One group includes words that allude to the sound of praise: "to sing," "to play," "to exult," "to make a joyful noise" (the last word denotes either the battle cry or the cry with which God or a king is hailed), and probably also *hillel,* "to praise" —a word which is well known as part of the expression "alleluia," properly *hallelu-yah,* "praise ye Yah[weh] (the Lord)." The other group contains words that denote the proclamation or exaltation of certain qualities of God, e.g., *romem,* "to exalt," *giddel,* "to magnify," *kibbed,* "to glorify," *berek,* "to bless." God is exalted, great, and glorious, and he is himself the source of all blessing; but the proclamation of these attributes makes them known to more and more people and thus confirms the worshiper's faith in the God who possesses them. God does not himself become greater or more exalted, but his attributes stand out more clearly to the worshipers, and thus he receives more of the glory that is due him. Of course, it is impossible to "bless" God in the sense that human beings can be blessed, for man cannot give blessing to God. But man can acknowledge God as the giver of all blessing, and praise him accordingly. Thus to bless God becomes synonymous with praising him. A good instance of

this interaction is to be found in Ps. 134:2,3: "Bless the Lord.
May the Lord bless you from Zion."[9]

But if thanksgiving is for the pious Israelite a kind of
praise, it should be a purely spontaneous act which could
never be described as an obligation or a duty. This is, for
the most part, the case, but there are a few instances where
the thought is expressed that man *ought* to thank God. Psalm
107 begins with an exhortation to give thanks to the Lord,
which is motivated by recounting instances of divine intervention in history and in the lives of individuals; it ends
with a sentence that sounds like a summary of the psalm:
"Whoever is wise, let him give heed to these things; let men
consider the steadfast love of the Lord" (Ps. 107:43). Is this
not as much as to say that a man who gives heed to God's
works realizes that it is his duty to give thanks to him? In
Ps. 9:13,14 the psalmist asks God to help him *in order that*
he may "recount his praises." If God helps in order to be
praised, it must be man's duty to respond to this intention.
Something similar is expressed in the well-known words:

> "Call upon me in the day of trouble;
> I will deliver you, and you shall glorify me."
> —*Ps. 50:15*

When God keeps his promise and delivers the psalmist, the
latter is expected to praise God in return. Reading between
the lines of Psalm 106, we see how bad it is not to consider
God's wonderful works, or not to remember the abundance
of his steadfast love (vs. 7), or to forget God, the Saviour, and
the great things and wondrous works he has done (vss. 2,22).
It is easy to see how faith and praise in Ps. 106:12 are contrasted with forgetting God's works in vs. 13. It is the same
idea that is so marvelously expressed in Deuteronomy, when
Israel is told not to let the abundance of the promised land
make them forget to give God thanks for it all (Deut. 6:10-12;
8:7-18). This is another example of the theocentric attitude

of the psalmists; when God intervenes to help, man should not put himself at the center of things and simply rejoice that he is saved; he should rather give God the glory. Failure to do this would be arrogance, not letting God be God.

A special aspect of this requirement of praise and thanksgiving is revealed in those psalms of lament that contain a vow of praise or thanksgiving. At times the psalmist also promises to offer sacrifices:

> He will requite my enemies with evil;
> in thy faithfulness put an end to them.
> With a free-will offering I will sacrifice to thee;
> I will give thanks to thy name, O Lord, for it is good.
> —*Ps. 54:5,6*

On other occasions he only vows to offer praise:

> Bring me out of prison,
> that I may give thanks to thy name!
> —*Ps. 142:7*

We should not think that this represents simply a sort of bargaining between the psalmist and God: If you help me, I will give you praise. This is no *do ut des* attitude: "I give in order that you may give." "But he who, crying to God out of the depths, is concerned not with his own distress but with God, he knows that his praise and his vow belong together with his crying. He knows that all is not done when he has said his prayer and God has heard it and granted him help. Something more must come after that. He knows that he owes God something. The vow gives weight and dignity to his prayer. He knows that with the vow that he adds to his prayer a history between himself and God begins."[10]

The place for thanksgiving and praise is the temple:

> Enter his gates with thanksgiving,
> and his courts[11] with praise!
> Give thanks to him, bless his name!
> —*Ps. 100:4*

> Praise the Lord!
> Praise God in his sanctuary!
> —*Ps. 150:1*[12]

The thanksgiving and praise is offered before the congregation:

> With my mouth I will give great thanks to the Lord;
> I will praise him in the midst of the throng.
> —*Ps. 109:30*

It is noteworthy that the phrase "I will give thanks," or "I will praise," very rarely stands alone; it is most frequently combined with an exhortation to fellow worshipers: "O give thanks," "Praise the Lord" (see, e.g., Ps. 118:1,21,28,29). Praise and thanksgiving are not a private matter; they are the concern of the whole congregation:

> I will bless the Lord at all times;
> his praise shall continually be in my mouth.
> . . . .
> O magnify the Lord with me,
> and let us exalt his name together!
> —*Ps. 34:1,3*

In this way the worshiping community is united in the praise of the Lord, and a fellowship in thanksgiving and praise is created. Thus through the experience of common worship the sense of God's greatness and exaltation is enhanced.

If we would grasp the central motif in the psalmists' praise of the Lord, we shall have to pay attention to the reasons they cite in their exhortations to praise and thanksgiving. As a rule the psalms begin with such exhortations as "praise," "give thanks," "bless," and these are followed by a reason beginning with *ki*, "for." Sometimes the whole psalm provides the motivation to respond to the initial exhortation.

In a few cases we hear only that "it is good" to thank or to praise the Lord:

It is good to give thanks to the Lord,
to sing praises to thy name, O Most High.
                                        —*Ps. 92:1*

Praise the Lord!
For it is good to sing praises to our God;
for he is gracious, and a song of praise is seemly.
                                        —*Ps. 147:1*

The question is: What does *tob,* "good," mean in this connection? According to some scholars, it is simply equivalent to "right" or "appropriate," which might be supported by the expression "it is seemly" in the latter quotation. But it should also be remembered that *tob* means both "good" and "beautiful." It has even been said that in these verses the aesthetic and the religio-ethical elements of the cultic experience are combined. It is also possible to interpret such expressions psychologically: it feels good to praise the Lord, for in doing so one experiences joy and satisfaction. This interpretation could be supported by a variant translation of Ps. 147:1: "It is good to sing praises to our Lord, yea, it is pleasant, and a song of praise is seemly," a translation which is admissible in terms of the original unpunctuated Hebrew text. In that case there would be reference in this passage to an emotional experience. But it is hardly possible to know for certain which aspect of "good" was originally intended. Perhaps even a combination of two or more connotations of the word could have been in the psalmist's mind.

In most cases, as was indicated, the reason for praise and thanksgiving is introduced by the particle "for." The wording of this motivation can be quite general, such as a reference to God's goodness, mercy, and faithfulness:

O give thanks to the Lord, for he is good;
his steadfast love endures for ever!
                                        —*Ps. 118:1*

> For the Lord is good;
> his steadfast love endures for ever,
> and his faithfulness to all generations.
> —*Ps. 100:5*[13]

Sometimes there is a reference to God's mighty deeds:

> Who can utter the mighty doings of the Lord,
> or show forth all his praise?   —*Ps. 106:2*

In other psalms the psalmist goes on to explain more fully the reason for his thanksgiving, telling of a specific event that he regards as a divine intervention, or of the wonders of nature, or of God's marvelous acts in the history of the chosen people.

If the reference is to a special event, we are rarely told of it in concrete detail. The psalmist puts his thanksgiving in very general terms. He is not primarily interested in describing what actually happened. His main concern is to interpret it as an instance of divine intervention, and to confess and proclaim that God has acted.[14] Consequently, we do not know exactly what occasioned the psalmist's gratitude. Some examples will illustrate this:

> Blessed be the Lord!
> for he has heard the voice of my supplications.
> The Lord is my strength and my shield;
> in him my heart trusts;
> so I am helped, and my heart exults,
> and with my song I give thanks to him.
> —*Ps. 28:6,7*

The Lord has heard and answered the psalmist's prayer, but we are not told what God has actually done. Verse 8 seems to indicate that the speaker is a king ("his anointed"), and the beginning of the psalm contains a prayer for the punishment of the "wicked." It is possible, therefore, that some triumph over enemies is involved. But the essential thing is not the nature of the danger or of the divine help, but the psalmist's recognition that he was helped by God in answer to his prayer. Thus the psalm bears witness to his dependence on God.

> O magnify the Lord with me,
> and let us exalt his name together!
> I sought the Lord, and he answered me,
> and delivered me from all my fears.
> . . . .
> This poor man cried, and the Lord heard him,
> and saved him out of all his troubles.
>
> —Ps. 34:3,4,6

In this case the psalmist does not give the slightest hint as to the details of his distress and deliverance, but the emphasis is exclusively on the fact that God has answered his prayer. It is also characteristic that he asks his fellow worshipers to join him in his thanksgiving.

> My vows to thee I must perform, O God;
> I will render thank offerings to thee,
> For thou hast delivered my soul from death,
> yea, my feet from falling,
> that I may walk before God
> in the light of life.   —Ps. 56:12,13

Here because of a vow the psalmist's thanksgiving is an obligation, but it is no burdensome duty, for he knows that he has been saved from death. (Similarly in Ps. 86:12,13: "I give thanks to thee . . . for thou hast delivered my soul from the depths of Sheol.") It is true that death and Sheol do not have to be taken literally, since they belong to the traditional imagery of the psalms of lament. But it is nevertheless clear that the psalmist regards what has happened to him as a manifestation of God's power over all forces hostile to life. It is God alone and no human being who can give help in such a situation. When this is realized, thanksgiving becomes a matter of course. The details are unimportant. The essential thing is that God has achieved the impossible; even death has had to yield its prey.

In Psalm 92 we again find a general expression:

> It is good to give thanks to the Lord.
>
> . . . .
>
> For thou, O Lord, hast made me glad by thy work;
> at the works of thy hands I sing for joy.—*Ps. 92:1,4*

But farther on in the psalm we get more information:

> For, lo, thy enemies shall perish;
> all evildoers shall be scattered.
> *—Ps. 92:9*

This indicates that the psalmist is giving thanks because of a triumph over enemies, but we are not told what sort of enemies they are. Again, the essential thing is the religious evaluation: victory is God's deed, not man's achievement.

However, in all these cases it is a specific event that has caused the thanksgiving. These are, in other words, instances of "narrative praise." The psalmist has interpreted a specific event as a divine act—often as an answer to prayer—and his thanksgiving is his profession of this interpretation, or rather of the God whose power and goodness he has discovered in the event.

Strangely enough, the reference is not very often to "spiritual" gifts; earthly and material things are, instead, given a religious interpretation. There are a few exceptions:

> Bless the Lord, O my soul;
> and all that is within me, bless his holy name!
> Bless the Lord, O my soul,
> and forget not all his benefits,
> who forgives all your iniquity,
> who heals all your diseases,
> who redeems your life from the Pit,
> who crowns you with steadfast love and mercy.
> *—Ps. 103:1-4*

Even if we are not able to tell precisely what the psalmist means by redemption from the Pit (i.e., the grave, or Sheol) or by being crowned with love and mercy, it is obvious that the chief emphasis is on the forgiveness of sins and not on any particular experience of deliverance from some particular danger. There may even be in vs. 3 an allusion to the close connection assumed between disease and sin: the forgiveness of sins and the healing of diseases appeared to the psalmist as almost identical. We remember that illness was regarded as potential death and recovery as being rescued from Sheol. It should be added that this psalm has nothing in it to indicate its origin in a particular situation; it is rather a hymn written for use in the temple at some religious festival, perhaps the great New Year's festival.

We turn now to the second type of praise, "descriptive" praise. Psalm 104 begins in exactly the same way as Psalm 103: "Bless the Lord, O my soul," but the sequel is entirely different. The motivation for praise is not a single event or God's goodness toward a single individual, but the creation of the world. First there is a description of God's creative work in the beginning, how he stretched out the sky like a tent, set the earth on its foundations, and appointed a place for the waters. Then follows an enthusiastic description of God's constant care for all that he has created, both men and animals; it is emphasized that all of God's creatures are entirely dependent on him.

A similar theme is expressed in Psalm 148. Here heaven, the sun, and the stars are all called upon to praise the Lord:

> Let them praise the name of the Lord!
> For he commanded and they were created.
> And he established them for ever and ever;
> he fixed their bounds which cannot be passed.
>
> —*Ps. 148:5,6*

God has created order in the world; everything has its fixed place and everything follows the order established by God in the beginning. This is the Israelitic counterpart to our concept of the laws of nature. This gives the Israelite a feeling of security in a world where, according to his belief, chaotic powers threaten to disturb the established order whenever God does not restrain them. We rely upon the physical laws inherent in nature and expect all things to behave according to these laws. The Israelite knew that everything was in the hands of God and was dependent on him. If he withdrew his protection, the world would be thrown into complete chaos. That is why the Israelite thanked and praised God for establishing the order of creation. The same idea is expressed in the following lines:

> Praise is due to thee, O God, in Zion;
> and to thee shall vows be performed,
> O thou who hearest prayer!
> To thee shall all flesh come.
> . . . .
> who by thy strength hast established the mountains,
> being girded with might;
> who dost still the roaring of the seas,
> the roaring of their waves,
> the tumult of the peoples.   —*Ps. 65:1,2,6,7*

The mountains, the firmest things of all on this earth, stand immovable only because of the power of the Creator. It was he who in the beginning subdued the rebellious waters and assigned to them their place. The same God is able to subjugate the nations of the world that are hostile to God and to his people Israel.

"By dread thou dost answer us in deliverance," says the same psalmist (Ps. 65:5).

Psalm 136 begins with the usual exhortation to thank God and then describes the acts of creation:

O give thanks to the Lord, for he is good,
for his steadfast love endures for ever.

. . . .
to him who by understanding made the heavens,

. . . .
to him who spread out the earth upon the waters,

. . . .
to him who made the great lights,

. . . .
the sun . . . ,

. . . .
the moon and stars.   —*Ps. 136:1,5-9*

But then the psalmist goes on to describe God's acts in history:

To him who smote the first-born of Egypt,

. . . .
and brought Israel out from among them,

. . . .
with a strong hand and an outstretched arm,

. . . .
to him who led his people through the wilderness,

. . . .
a heritage to Israel his servant.
                                   —*Ps. 136:10-12,16,22*[15]

This is the constant source of gratitude for Israel: that the Lord delivered her from Egypt and led her into the promised land.

Praise the Lord, for the Lord is good;
sing to his name, for he is gracious!
For the Lord has chosen Jacob for himself,
Israel as his own possession.
For I know that the Lord is great,
and that our Lord is above all gods.—*Ps. 135:3-5*

Yahweh, the greatest and mightiest of all gods, the Creator and Lord of all the world, has chosen the people of Israel to be his peculiar people. Israel is his people and he is Israel's God: on this foundation all religious life in Israel rests. It is true that this consciousness of being elected could easily give rise to national pride. Yet as long as Israel remembered that her election was not due to her great numbers or her excellent qualities, but was due exclusively to the love of the Lord (Deut. 7:7, 8), it was recognized that humble gratitude was the proper attitude. "It is he that made us, and we are his;[16] we are his people, and the sheep of his pasture" (Ps. 100:3). Both as individuals and as a nation the pious of Israel owe their existence to the Lord, and as members of God's people they always feel surrounded by his care and protection.

A good summary of these ideas is given in Psalm 95:

> For the Lord is a great God,
> and a great King above all gods.
> In his hand are the depths of the earth;
> the heights of the mountains are his also.
> The sea is his, for he made it;
> for his hands formed the dry land.
> O come, let us worship and bow down,
> let us kneel before the Lord, our Maker!
> For he is our God,
> and we are the people of his pasture,
> and the sheep of his hand.
> —*Ps. 95:3-7*

It stands to reason that such an expression of worship is primarily the concern of the whole nation, or at any rate of the cult community. But it is also of great significance to the individual. As a matter of fact, it is as a member of the chosen people that the individual has fellowship with God. It is through the fellowship of God's peculiar people that he shares in the election and the promises of the covenant: "You shall be my people, and I shall be your God." This is probably a partial explanation for the strong emphasis on fellowship that we have observed in Israelitic religion. Through sharing the same holy history, in which the Lord has continuously manifested his grace and faithfulness, the Israelites' trust in God is strengthened. It is characteristic that the author of Psalm 22 seeks support for his faith and hope through recalling (in vss. 4, 5) God's help to his fathers. Participation in the same heritage also unites the believers with one another in their relationship to God.

But the creation and the exodus from Egypt were not only great and precious memories treasured by the faithful and now and then recollected or commemorated. They were events that were actualized and re-experienced whenever the great festivals were celebrated in the temple. The Feast of Tabernacles (or New Year's festival) had as its theme creation and the judgment (i.e., defeat) of God's enemies. The Passover festival made the exodus a living reality every year. It is certainly against this background that we should understand such a verse as Ps. 75:1:

> We give thanks to thee, O God; we give thanks.
> Thy name is near; they recount thy wondrous deeds.

This psalm belongs to the New Year's festival and its theme is the judgment of God's enemies. The introductory verse indicates something of the sentiment that prevailed during the celebration. There was thanksgiving to God, because his presence was felt when his wonderful deeds were remembered.

Another psalm that belonged to the same festival and also deals with the defeat of the enemies provides another illustration of the mood in which the feast was celebrated:

> Blessed be the Lord,
> who daily bears us up;
> God is our salvation.
> Our God is a God of salvation;
> and to God, the Lord, belongs escape from death.
> —*Ps. 68:19,20*

From the time that the Lord originally chose Israel, he has "borne" his people and been their helper. He has given them "salvation," which in this context could almost mean "victory." He is able to rescue them even from the utmost danger and distress ("death"). All this becomes a living and present reality for those who witness God's triumph in the cultic drama.

Another theme for thanksgiving is rain, fertility, and rich harvests:

> Thou visitest the earth and waterest it,
> thou greatly enrichest it;
> the river of God is full of water;
> thou providest their grain,
> for so thou hast prepared it.
> Thou waterest its furrows abundantly,
> settling its ridges,
> softening it with showers,
> and blessing its growth.
> Thou crownest the year with thy bounty;
> the tracks of thy chariot drip with fatness.
> The pastures of the wilderness drip,
> the hills gird themselves with joy,
> the meadows clothe themselves with flocks,
> the valleys deck themselves with grain,
> they shout and sing together for joy.
> *—Ps. 65:9-13*

This enthusiastic and poetically impressive description of the beneficial effect of the rain leaves no doubt about the great joy and gratitude that fills the heart of the psalmist. Rain and fertility are God's gifts, and if we remember how scarce rain is in Palestine, we easily understand the enthusiasm of this hymn of praise. We should not depreciate the interest expressed in this psalm for "material" things. What is essential is that this material benefit is regarded as coming from God. The Israelite does not distinguish in terms of value between material and spiritual benefits. Everything comes from God and is therefore equally valued. Hence it is also appropriate to thank God for every gift that is received.

91

CHAPTER 8

Myth and History

WE HAVE SEEN that God's creation of the world and his activity in the history of Israel were the themes of praise and thanksgiving at the great annual festivals. We also found that these themes were not only recited and celebrated in hymns, but they were also visualized and, in a way, re-enacted in the ritual acts of the cult. Unfortunately, we know nothing of the details of these festivals, so it is difficult to reconstruct the impact the various ceremonies must have had on the religious experience of the participants. Yet the sentiment of rejoicing that pervades the festival hymns is unmistakable:

> Hark, glad songs of victory
> in the tents of the righteous.
> —*Ps. 118:15*

> Blessed are the people who know the festal shout,
> ....
> who exult in thy name all the day. —*Ps. 89:15,16*

Heaven and earth are asked to join in the exultation and "joyful noise" of the festival (Pss. 96:11 f.; 98:7; 148). There is an illuminating passage in the Book of Isaiah which shows what a religious festival meant to the worshipers:

> You shall have a song
> as in the night when a holy feast is kept;
> and gladness of heart,

> as when one sets out to the sound of the flute
> to go to the mountain of the Lord,
> to the Rock of Israel.   —*Isa. 30:29*

Thus singing and music, joy and gladness are regarded as the most characteristic features of such a celebration. This rejoicing is due to the fact that the worshipers "go up to the Lord, the Rock of Israel." In other words, it cannot be separated from the experience of the Lord's presence in the sanctuary, especially during the time of the celebration of the festival.

For some time now one festival particularly has drawn the attention of Old Testament scholars. It has been variously called the enthronement festival, the New Year's festival, or the covenant festival,[1] and there has been considerable difference of opinion as to its character and special meaning. As a matter of fact, it was probably nothing but one aspect of the pre-exilic Feast of Tabernacles. The main elements of the festival have been tentatively reconstructed on the basis of the so-called enthronement psalms which deal with the kingship of Yahweh, the creation of the world, and the defeat or "judgment" of enemies and rebellious nations. (It should be emphasized that these psalms have nothing to do with the royal psalms connected with the enthronement of a king of Israel, such as Psalms 2 and 110. It is Yahweh who is celebrated as the King of the world, and whether this is to be called an enthronement or not is a matter of controversy.[2] God, having in reality always been King of the universe, does not *become* King through the rites of the festival; it is just that the celebration of his kingship finds expression in formulae that otherwise belong to enthronement ceremonies.)

The psalms in question are among those best known and most appreciated in the Christian church, which is another reason why we should give them special attention, even though it is impossible to determine in detail their original significance for the individual worshiper. Moreover, they shed light on another question about which there has recently been a great deal of debate, namely, the question of myth and history.[3]

Discussion of this question has often been confused for lack of a clear definition of the exact meaning of the word "myth." In everyday speech a myth often means a story in which gods (and goddesses) appear as acting characters. It is also generally understood that a myth is not true. Modern writers on comparative religion, however, tend to use the word "myth" in a very specific sense. They define "myth" as "the spoken part of a ritual": in a cultic celebration the myth explains the rite, and the rite visualizes or enacts the myth.[4] According to this definition, such a story as the account of Israel's exodus from Egypt would be a myth, since the Lord appears as one of the main characters, and the story forms an integrating part of the celebration of Passover. At the same time the majority of scholars maintain that this narrative reflects a real historical event.

How is this problem of the relation of myth and history to be solved? For our purpose the best solution would be to find an unambiguous answer in the psalms themselves. Perhaps our difficulty arises from the fact that we are making distinctions which were not intended by the psalmists. We may as well begin our discussion with an examination of the enthronement psalms.

As has already been stated, the creation of the world is here one of the principal motifs. But, in contrast to the creation story in Genesis, chapter 1, creation, as a rule, is not viewed in these psalms as resulting solely from God's creative word. Instead, it is achieved through God's fierce struggle with chaotic powers represented by the half-personified Sea or Deep (or primeval ocean):

Thou didst set the earth on its foundations,
so that it should never be shaken.
Thou didst cover it with the deep as with a garment;[5]
the waters stood above the mountains.
At thy rebuke they fled;
at the sound of thy thunder they took to flight.
The mountains rose, the valleys sank down
to the place which thou didst appoint for them.
Thou didst set a bound which they should not pass,
so that they might not again cover the earth.

—*Ps. 104:5-9*

The word for "deep," *tehom,* corresponds exactly to the name of the dragon in the Babylonian myth of creation, Tiamat. This dragon was defeated by Marduk after a terrible battle, and the world was created out of its body. In the psalm this mythological element has been largely suppressed. "The deep" is more or less equivalent to "the waters," i.e., the masses of water that were believed in the beginning to have covered the earth. Yet these waters are conceived of as a semi-personal being, which flees at the rebuke of God and which will never more transgress the border that he has set for it. This drawing of a boundary between the waters and the dry land is the necessary condition for the existence of the present world.

There are passages in which the mythological is more strongly evident, as, e.g., the following passage from Psalm 89:

Thou dost rule the raging of the sea;
when its waves rise, thou stillest them.
Thou didst crush Rahab like a carcass,
thou didst scatter thy enemies with thy mighty arm.
The heavens are thine, the earth also is thine;
the world and all that is in it, thou hast founded them.
The north and the south, thou hast created them;
Tabor and Hermon joyously praise thy name.

—*Ps. 89:9-12*

Here it is obviously not only the Sea or the Deep which has been defeated by the Lord; it is a mythological being, Rahab, that has been crushed (or "pierced," another possible meaning of the word). It is also apparent that this victory is connected with the creation and with God's dominion over heaven and earth. It seems that here we are entitled to speak of a myth. But we must ask: What is the religious significance of this myth? What did it mean for the pious Israelite who heard it recited and perhaps even saw it enacted symbolically in the cult?

Before we try to answer these questions, it might be helpful to quote another passage from the Psalms:

> The earth is the Lord's and the fulness thereof,
> the world and those who dwell therein;
> for he has founded it upon the seas,
> and established it upon the rivers. —*Ps. 24:1, 2*

According to the Israelitic view, the earth was a flat disk, floating on the ocean (*tehom*) and supported by firm mountains rooted in the depths of the sea. Therefore the psalmist says, "The world is established and shall never be moved" (Pss. 93:1; 96:10). Knowing this, the Israelite felt secure in this world. The earth is established and shall not be moved, because it rests in God's hand and all the forces of chaos and death and disorder are restrained by his power. Everything has received its place and its function: "He set a law for them which cannot be transgressed" (Ps. 148:6). Consequently, the doctrine of creation is not primarily a theoretical statement about the origin of the world, about something that happened long ago. It is rather a proclamation of a present reality; creation means that the evil powers are defeated and that the order of the world is established for ever. This is what affords security to man as he lives in God's world. Creation, therefore, is also a redemptive act, the results of which are still present and form a constant source of joy and gratitude, especially on the occasions when they are commemorated in the cult.

God's creative activity is not completed; it is still going on. It is he who makes the rain to fall, so that the earth produces grass, plants, wine, and oil for the benefit of men and animals (Ps. 104:13-18). Night and day each have their place in his plan for the world (Ps. 104:19-23; cf. Ps. 74:16 f.). The forces of nature obey him, and he cares for men and animals; they are all dependent on him:

> These all look to thee,
> to give them their food in due season.
> When thou givest to them, they gather it up;
> when thou openest thy hand, they are filled with good things.
> When thou hidest thy face, they are dismayed;
> when thou takest away their breath, they die
> and return to their dust.
> When thou sendest forth thy Spirit, they are created;
> and thou renewest the face of the ground.   —*Ps. 104:27-30*

For the individual this concept of creation has a twofold significance. On one hand, man stands before his God in respectful gratitude because he is so "wonderfully made" (Ps. 139:14, KJV) and because all his days are known and predetermined by God (Ps. 139:16). Or he may feel his transitoriness and his insignificance before the Eternal One:

> Thou turnest man back to the dust,
> and sayest, "Turn back, O children of men!"
> —*Ps. 90:3*

This passage and the verses just quoted from Psalm 104 express the feeling of absolute dependence on God that has often been regarded as the essential feature of all true religion.

Contemplating the greatness of creation the psalmist feels his own smallness and turns his eyes toward God, the Creator:

97

> When I look at thy heavens, the work of thy fingers,
> the moon and the stars which thou hast established;
> what is man that thou art mindful of him,
> and the son of man that thou dost care for him?
>
> —*Ps. 8:3,4*

The "man" or "son of man" referred to in this passage may be Adam, the king,[6] or man in general; but the religious experience, in any case, remains the same.

On the other hand, this God before whom man feels so weak and insignificant is the ultimate ground of the universe, man's eternal refuge:

> Lord, thou hast been our dwelling place
> in all generations.
> Before the mountains were brought forth,
> or ever thou hadst formed the earth and the world,
> from everlasting to everlasting thou art God.
>
> —*Ps. 90:1,2*

As for man, his days are like grass;
he flourishes like a flower of the field;
for the wind passes over it, and it is gone,
and its place knows it no more.
But the steadfast love of the Lord is from everlasting to everlasting.

> —*Ps. 103:15-17*

The sudden withering of the grass and the flowers from the heat of the sun and the burning desert wind provides an impressive contrast to the only thing that remains: God and his steadfast love.

But the continuing activity of the Creator is not limited to the world of nature. It is just as clearly visible in the events of history, especially in God's gracious dealings with his chosen people. There are a number of psalms that deal with the history of Israel, interpreting this history as the product of God's activity. History, so understood, can be used to teach the psalmist's hearers to know their God. Psalms 78, 105, and 106 are cases in point. These psalms admittedly do not give the impression of being real cultic hymns; they seem rather to be based on meditation and reflection upon a cultic motif. Yet it is possible that they were used in the temple. Psalm 81 is also a psalm of this type, although in this case the beginning of the psalm is clearly cultic, speaking of joy and rejoicing at a temple festival.[7] Then God himself speaks in an oracle ("I hear a voice I had not known"):

> "I relieved your shoulder of the burden;
> your hands were freed from the basket.
> In distress you called, and I delivered you;
> I answered you in the secret place of thunder."
> —*Ps. 81:6,7*

The psalmist goes on to consider the history of his people, evaluating it in the light of his religious insight. His view of history is the one we find in the so-called Deuteronomic writings of the Old Testament: Joshua, Judges, Samuel, Kings. He stresses the interaction of the people's religious attitude and their destiny: sin calls for punishment; repentance is the way to restoration. The essential point is that history is, so to speak, God's workshop. The history of Israel is a series of divine acts which began with the deliverance from Egypt, when God's victorious power was supremely manifested.

In a passage which we have already discussed in another connection, the remembrance of this great event is combined with a reference to seeing what God has done:

> Come and see what God has done:
> he is terrible in his deeds among men.
> He turned the sea into dry land;
> men passed through the river on foot.
> —*Ps. 66:5,6*

The miraculous event of the exodus is, as it were, a present reality; the worshipers in the temple see it and rejoice over it as if it had just taken place. It is present in their minds; they experience it anew; it occurs here and now. Similarly, a some-what obscure passage in Psalm 68 refers to the revelation at Mount Sinai in terms that indicate a renewed actualization of the event: "The Lord comes [or "came"] from Sinai into the holy place" (Ps. 68:17b). He is present in the temple and speaks to the congregation just as he did from the mountain. He establishes his covenant with the people anew just as he did long ago through Moses.

A similar point of view is expressed in a passage in Deu-teronomy: "The Lord our God made a covenant with us in Horeb. Not with our fathers did the Lord make this cove-nant, but with us who are all of us here alive this day. The Lord spoke with you face to face at the mountain out of the midst of the fire" (Deut. 5:2-4). "Not with our fathers . . . but with us": the covenant is a present reality.[8] So also Moses' speech in Deuteronomy, chapter 29, includes the following words: " 'You stand this day all of you before the Lord your God; . . . that you may enter into the sworn covenant of the Lord your God, which the Lord your God makes with you this day; that he may establish you this day as his people, and that he may be your God' " (Deut. 29:10,12,13). The cove-nant was established long ago at Mount Sinai, and yet Moses says that God is now making the same covenant with the people this day. This is a typical expression of Israelitic piety. That which happened once with basic significance for the religious community is still present in its consequences, and the commemoration of the event renews these consequences in the faith of the worshipers.

Something comparable is the case with respect to the Jewish celebration of Passover. The ritual still used today includes the recitation of a formula according to which every Jew is to regard himself as if he—and not his forefathers long ago—had come out of Egypt. Nor is the Christian church entirely un-familiar with this way of thinking. The Negro spiritual "Were

You There When They Crucified My Lord?" contains the same feeling of being contemporaneous with the remembered event, and a well-known Christmas carol asks the faithful to come to Bethlehem to behold and adore the King of angels. In both instances historic events that took place long ago are experienced as present in the imagination of the poet. The difference between this and the cultic re-enactment in ancient Israel is one of degree rather than of kind.

The exodus from Egypt was of basic significance for the faith of Israel and for their consciousness of being God's peculiar people. The covenant between Yahweh and the people was established through the events at Mount Sinai. But for the cultic community these were more than merely past events and historical memories. The effects and consequences of these events to the worshiping community were still present as the source from which the individual derived his strength and confidence:

> In thee our fathers trusted;
> they trusted, and thou didst deliver them.
> To thee they cried, and were saved;
> in thee they trusted, and were not disappointed.
> —*Ps. 22:4,5*

But, more than this, the deliverance from Egyptian slavery was conceived in terms that make it comparable to the act of creation. Psalm 74, a prayer for help in a situation in which enemies have destroyed and defiled the temple,[9] recalls God's former beneficent acts:

> Yet God my King is from of old,
> working salvation in the midst of the earth.
> Thou didst divide the sea by thy might;
> thou didst break the heads of the dragons on the waters.
> Thou didst crush the heads of Leviathan,
> thou didst give him as food for the creatures of the wilderness.
> Thou didst cleave open springs and brooks;

thou didst dry up ever-flowing streams.
Thine is the day, thine also the night;
. . . .
thou hast fixed all the bounds of the earth;
thou hast made summer and winter.   —*Ps. 74:12-17*

The dividing of the sea could refer either to the crossing of
the Red Sea or to the defeat of the personified primeval Sea
in the creation. The breaking of the heads of the dragons
and of Leviathan reminds us of the monster of the creation
myth, while the drying up of streams seems to allude to the
exodus or to the crossing of the Jordan under Joshua. The
last verses again refer to the order of creation. Obviously it
was felt that the same imagery which was used to describe the
creation of the world could also be used to describe historical
events involving the defeat of hostile powers.

While there may be some doubt as to the correct interpretation of the mythological images in Psalm 74, it is entirely
clear in the following passage that what is meant is the
exodus:

> Thou art the God who workest wonders,
> who hast manifested thy might among the peoples.
> Thou didst with thy arm redeem thy people,
> the sons of Jacob and Joseph.
> When the waters saw thee, O God,
> when the waters saw thee, they were afraid,
> yea, the deep trembled.
> The clouds poured out water;
> the skies gave forth thunder;
> thy arrows flashed on every side.
> The crash of thy thunder was in the whirlwind;
> thy lightnings lighted up the world;
> the earth trembled and shook.
> Thy way was through the sea,
> thy path through the great waters;
> yet thy footprints were unseen.
> Thou didst lead thy people like a flock
> by the hand of Moses and Aaron.   —*Ps. 77:14-20*

It is obvious that this mythological description refers to the exodus and the deliverance from Egypt. This historical event is represented as a grandiose theophany, described according to the traditional pattern.

There is a similar combination of God's power in nature and in the exodus in another psalm:

> Whatever the Lord pleases he does,
> in heaven and on earth,
> in the seas and all deeps.
> He it is who makes the clouds rise at the end of the earth,
> who makes lightnings for the rain
> and brings forth the wind from his storehouses.
> He it was who smote the first-born of Egypt,
> both of man and of beast;
> who in thy midst, O Egypt,
> sent signs and wonders
> against Pharaoh and all his servants;
> who smote many nations
> and slew mighty kings,
>
> . . . .
> and gave their land as a heritage,
> a heritage to his people Israel.   —*Ps. 135:6-10,12*

The implication is obviously that the Creator and Lord of the world has chosen the people of Israel, using all of his power to carry out his purpose. But there is a deeper congruence between the creation and the exodus: both involve God's victory over hostile powers. All those who oppose the Lord's plans for Israel are in the same category as the primeval chaotic powers at the dawn of creation.

The deliverance from Egypt, as we saw in Psalm 74, is an act of redemption that can be described in the same mythical categories as the creation, namely, as a battle against a dragon. The creation was God's first and decisive victory over the powers of chaos, and therefore also an act of redemption. On the other hand, the deliverance from Egypt was an act of

103

creation, a new victory over the evil powers and a new creation of the people. But just as God always maintains the order of creation and cares for all his creatures, so he also cares particularly for his people. He manifests himself in their history by punishing them, and also by forgiving their sins (Ps. 99:8). This divine activity, in turn, is also reflected in the political destinies of the nation of Israel.

In this way creation and redemption merge into a higher unity, which receives its character from a dynamic view of the world as a place where life and death, light and darkness, cosmos and chaos, the Lord and his enemies are engaged in constant struggle. This is also where myth and history meet: history is described in mythical categories, because it is Yahweh, the God of Israel, who is the main character in its drama.

In the history of Israel God's redemptive activity is especially manifested in the revelation of his word to his people. Thus Psalm 147 speaks of the creative words of God that produces snow and hail, wind and rain (Ps. 147:15-18), but then he goes on to mention the revealed word of God:

> He declares his word to Jacob,
> his statutes and ordinances to Israel.
> He has not dealt thus with any other nation;
> they do not know his ordinances.
> —*Ps. 147:19,20*

The words of the Lord given on Mount Sinai are, in a sense, another aspect of the creative word that maintains everything in the universe. Both are manifestations of the same divine will, both are aspects of the same divine order: the regular order of nature and the "righteousness" that should prevail in a healthy society.[10] God's law and the order of nature are two aspects of the same reality. Consequently, even if Psalm 19 is a composite of two originally separate psalms, the combination of the two is very meaningful. The heavens that tell

104

the glory of God and the firmament that proclaims his handi-
work, on one hand, and God's law that revives the soul, on
the other, are actually two manifestations of one and the same
divine will.

Elements of myth and history are combined in yet another
way in Psalm 89.[11] This long composition, containing varying
motifs, ends in a prayer for help for the Lord's anointed, i.e.,
for the king of Israel whom God has so cast off and rejected
that his enemies mock him and his throne has been cast to
the ground (Ps. 89:38-45). But the psalm begins with a song
of praise and an appeal to Yahweh as the Creator and the
Conqueror of Rahab (vss. 9-12). Then follows a reference,
not to the election of Israel and the exodus, but to the election of David as king of Israel:

> Of old thou didst speak in a vision
> to thy faithful one, and say:
> "I have set the crown upon one who is mighty,
> I have exalted one chosen from the people.
> I have found David, my servant;
> with my holy oil I have anointed him;
> so that my hand shall ever abide with him,
> my arm also shall strengthen him.
> The enemy shall not outwit him,
> the wicked shall not humble him.
> I will crush his foes before him
> and strike down those who hate him."
> —*Ps. 89:19-23*

In other words, David—and that means also more generally
the king of Israel—is appointed by the Lord himself to defeat
the enemies of Israel. He is to be the instrument through
which God realizes his own purposes in history.[12] Likewise,
Psalm 2, after describing the tumult of the nations and the
rebellion of the princes, points, in vss. 1-3, to the king whom
the Lord has installed on Mount Zion to rule with divine
authority as the one who is destined to crush the enemies

(Ps. 2:4-9). Rebellion against this king is rebellion against the
Lord himself (Ps. 2:2,11,12).

A similar attack by enemies is described in Psalm 48:

> For lo, the kings assembled,
> they came on together.
> As soon as they saw it, they were astounded,
> they were in panic, they took to flight;
> trembling took hold of them there,
> anguish as of a woman in travail.
> By the east wind thou didst shatter
> the ships of Tarshish.　　　　　*—Ps. 48:4-7*

We do not know what historical event is alluded to in these
verses, and it is even possible that, as in Psalm 2, no specific
historical event at all was being described by the psalmist.
Actually, it is hard to find a situation that corresponds to
either of these descriptions. Rather we have here the typical,
traditional, half-mythological expressions which are meant to
assert that no enemies, be they ever so strong, will be able to
do any serious harm to those who are on the Lord's side. This
interpretation may be further substantiated by the fact that
Ps. 48:8 seems to indicate that the whole scene could be observed in the temple or at least in Jerusalem.[13] In any case,
whether this victory was real or simply a typical representation of the Israelitic faith, it was obviously celebrated in the
temple and interpreted as a manifestation of divine help.

There are other psalms that use more concrete expressions.
In Ps. 83:6-9 a whole series of hostile nations is enumerated:
Edom, Moab, Ammon, Amalek, Philistines, Tyre, Assyria,
et cetera. However, here again it might be asked whether there
is any historical situation that fits the description of this coali-
tion. Here too we may have a traditional formula, a series of
typical expressions that are not applicable to one and the
same situation.[14]

But even if the national enemies are *described* in general

and typical terms, they are nevertheless real, and the essential point is that in all such cases Israel looked for help to the Lord, their God. For he was a God who was active in history, governing the destiny of his people. Therefore, it was to him that they owed all thanks for their victories—victories which were at once also victories over the representatives of the powers of chaos.

This explains why what we call myth and history are so often combined in the Psalms. History is represented in the form of "myth" in so far as Yahweh fights for Israel. Because Israel's enemies are also Yahweh's enemies, they are sometimes described in mythical terms. The background idea at this point is somewhat similar to what we found to be the case with respect to calamities: by fitting the enemies into a traditional pattern, labeling them, they can be interpreted from the religious point of view and placed within the total world view defined by faith.

To the Israelite myth and history are not essentially distinct from each other. In both it is God who acts to defeat the evil powers, at one and the same time creating and saving. The creation and the deliverance from Egypt are equivalent manifestations of God's power and grace. Both are also commemorated in the cult, one at the New Year's festival, the other at the Passover. Of particular interest is the combination in the New Year's festival—with which Psalm 89 is probably to be connected—of the creation motif with the idea of the king as chosen to be God's representative and instrument in Israel. As God's representative the king is to destroy the enemies of the nation; but since Israel is God's people, these enemies are also God's enemies.

CHAPTER 9

The Law and the Messiah

THERE ARE two elements of the religion of the Psalms that have not yet been touched upon in our investigation, though they have been of decisive importance for the subsequent development, namely, the law and the Messiah. We shall deal with these elements briefly in this concluding chapter.

We have learned to regard Judaism as a legalistic religion, or, perhaps more correctly, a religion of the law. Since the emphasis on the law, however, is post-exilic, we should not expect to find much of the later legalistic aspect of Judaism expressed in the Psalms, which are for the most part pre-exilic. Nevertheless, there are occasional references to the law in a few psalms, and in the earliest of these psalms the ethical obligations of the law and the cultic aspects of religion are usually closely related.

The generally accepted picture of Israelitic religion, based as it is primarily on the preaching of the great prophets, makes a sharp distinction between cult and ethics. Cult and ethics are thought to be mutually exclusive. The prophets, it is said, condemned cultic religion and called for a purely ethical faith. It is true, of course, that a one-sided emphasis on the cult may conceivably lead to neglect of the ethical commandments. But in such a psalm as Psalm 24 we learn that this is not necessarily so, and that originally in Israel cult and ethics were intimately connected.

To understand this psalm we have to imagine a situation somewhat like this: A procession approaches the gates of the temple, singing a hymn to the Creator of the world (Ps. 24: 1,2). There it stops and the question is asked:

> Who shall ascend the hill of the Lord?
> And who shall stand in his holy place?
> —*Ps. 24:3*

In other words, who is worthy to enter the temple? The answer is:

> He who has clean hands and a pure heart,
> who does not lift up his soul to what is false,[1]
> and does not swear deceitfully.   —*Ps. 24:4*

Then the gates are addressed and told to be lifted up to let in Yahweh, the King of glory. We do not know how God's presence was symbolized in the ceremony, but the context presupposes the fact that he was indeed thought to take part in it. Possibly the ark of the covenant was carried in the procession to symbolize his presence. Psalms of this kind, which set forth the conditions for entering the sanctuary, are often called "entrance liturgies" or entrance *torahs*. *Torah* is the common Hebrew word for "law." These entrance liturgies define the requirements for those who are to be admitted to the holy place and permitted to participate in the cult that is performed there. Since the requirements are of an ethical character, it is evident that in the Psalms there is no opposition between cult and ethics.

A more extensive entrance *torah* is to be found in Psalm 15:

> O Lord, who shall sojourn in thy tent?
> Who shall dwell on thy holy hill?
> He who walks blamelessly, and does what is right,

109

> and speaks truth from his heart;
> who does not slander with his tongue,
> and does no evil to his friend,
> nor takes up a reproach against his neighbor;
> . . . .
> but who honors those who fear the Lord;
> who swears to his own hurt and does not change;
> who does not put out his money at interest,
> and does not take a bribe against the innocent.
> He who does these things shall never be moved.
> —*Ps. 15:1-5*

Here too there are ethical requirements for those who are to participate in the cult. We notice that special emphasis is placed on justice and solidarity in social life.

It is probable that the Ten Commandments in some similar way had a place in the cult, perhaps as part of a ceremony of covenant renewal. It should be noted that the story of the giving of the law at Sinai includes a theophany—which, as we have seen, is a cultic element—and the consecration of the people—which seems to be a preparation for a cultic performance.

In the second part of Psalm 19 there is a hymn in praise of the law of the Lord, which has been added to a very ancient hymn to God as the Creator:

> The law of the Lord is perfect,
> reviving the soul;
> the testimony of the Lord is sure,
> making wise the simple;
> the precepts of the Lord are right,
> rejoicing the heart;
> the commandment of the Lord is pure,
> enlightening the eyes;
> the fear of the Lord is clean,
> enduring for ever;
> the ordinances of the Lord are true,
> and righteous altogether.

> More to be desired are they than gold,
> even much fine gold.
>
> . . . .
>
> Moreover by them is thy servant warned;
> in keeping them there is great reward.
>   —*Ps. 19:7-11*

This is not the place to discuss whether or not this part of the psalm is later than the introductory verses, though it may very well be later. But we should focus our attention on the appraisal given to the law. The Hebrew word for "law" means "instruction" or "showing the way."[2] In other words, the law reveals God's will and shows man the way he is to walk in obedience before his God. But the law is not regarded here as a list of difficult duties or as a heavy burden. On the contrary, it is a gracious illumination for man's welfare, an instruction in God's will for which the psalmist feels profound gratitude. He loves God's law and finds his joy in it. Whether the reference is to the codified law of the Pentateuch or to the living proclamation of the law in the cult, what really matters is the psalmist's attitude to the revelation of God's will.

The same enthusiastic love of the law is expressed in Psalm 1:

> Blessed is the man
>
> . . . .
>
> [whose] delight is in the law of the Lord,
> and on his law he meditates day and night.
>   —*Ps. 1:1,2*

This psalm is generally considered to be late and has possibly no connection with the temple cult. But it is obvious that the image of the tree planted by streams of water is old and has cultic associations. It has even been suggested that the psalm was originally a sort of "mirror for kings" which within the framework of the cult was meant to set before the king his duties and the consequences of his fulfilling or neglecting them.[3] As a matter of fact, Deuteronomy reflects a similar ideal for a king: the king is to have in his possession a copy of the law "and he shall read in it all the days of his life, that he may learn to fear the Lord his God, by keeping all the words of this law and these statutes, and doing them" (Deut. 17:19). However, it is hard to escape the impression that Psalm 1 represents a relatively late stage in the history of Israelitic religion. Its author has probably employed ancient motifs and phrases, but used them for his own purposes. In this psalm we have an example of religious poetry that reflects the beginnings of the legalistic piety of Judaism.

The same type of religion expresses itself at considerable length in Psalm 119, which in one hundred and seventy-six skillfully composed verses describes the psalmist's love for and joy in God's law and word. In each group of eight verses every verse begins with the same Hebrew letter; the groups themselves are arranged in the order of the alphabet to form the psalm. In each one of the eight verses within a group the author uses a new word for the divine revelation: "word," "law," "testimonies," "precepts," "statutes," "commandments," "ordinances." Here we have obviously left the temple cult behind. Here the law and the word have a value of their own, having been detached from their original connection with the covenant cult of Israel.

It is this legalistic religion that was further developed in Judaism, and opposed by Jesus and Paul, and it is this emphasis on the law that still characterizes present-day Judaism.

Another line of thought which developed in an entirely different way is represented in the royal psalms, those psalms that refer to the king of Israel and define his position as the representative or vicegerent of the Lord in Israel. In view of what we have said of the theocentricity of the Psalms it might seem strange that so many of them are devoted to the earthly king, the king of Israel "on Mount Zion." But in reality these psalms are also theocentric in nature. The king is the Lord's anointed, installed as king by God himself (Ps. 2:6):

> He [the Lord] said to me, "You are my son,
> today I have begotten you.
> Ask of me, and I will make the nations your heritage,
> and the ends of the earth your possession." —*Ps. 2:7,8*

Here it is God who acts; it is he who takes the initiative. He chooses the king; he installs him; he gives him his power and authority. It is also God who conquers the king's enemies:

> The Lord says to my lord:
> "Sit at my right hand,
> till I make your enemies your footstool."
> The Lord sends forth from Zion
> your mighty scepter.
> Rule in the midst of your foes!—*Ps. 110:1,2*

Similarly, when the king is described as a just and righteous ruler, Psalm 72 says:

> May he judge thy people with righteousness,
> and thy poor with justice!
> . . . .
> May he defend the cause of the poor of the people,
> give deliverance to the needy,
> and crush the oppressor!   —*Ps. 72:2,4*

It is nonetheless clear that his righteousness is given to him by God (Ps. 72:1).

Another psalm addresses the king on his wedding day in the following terms:

> In your majesty ride forth victoriously
> for the cause of truth and to defend the right;
> let your right hand teach you dread deeds!
> . . . .
> Your divine throne[4] endures for ever and ever.
> Your royal scepter is a scepter of equity;
> you love righteousness and hate wickedness.
> Therefore God, your God, has anointed you
> with the oil of gladness above your fellows.
>   —*Ps. 45:4,6,7*

The king is God's servant with the responsibility of maintaining justice and righteousness among God's people. His royal authority has been given to him by God so that he might accomplish God's will.

From the very beginning the Christian church understood these psalms as prophecies of Christ, and to a certain extent modern research has justified this interpretation. It has been shown that the messianic hope in Israel grew out of the idea of the king as the God-sent ruler. The royal psalms prepare the way for the Christian belief in the Messiah, and thus form an important and essential part of the history of revelation. As a matter of fact, the Christian belief in Jesus as the messianic King and Saviour would be unthinkable and unintelligible apart from the background of the Old Testament kingship ideology as expressed in the royal psalms.

Moreover, there is a group of psalms referring to the righteous sufferer (such as Pss. 22, 69, and others) in which the New Testament has also seen prophecies of Christ. It has been suggested that these were originally royal psalms, although it is difficult to adduce definite proof of this theory. If the theory is true, this would constitute another connecting link between the Psalms and the Christ of the New Testament.[5]

Yet the real reason why the Psalms have been and still are so highly appreciated by Christians is not their prophetical character. It is the fact that they contain expressions of timeless, living religion which is closely akin to that of the New Testament. The Psalms are at the same time profoundly human and profoundly religious. They express needs and hopes which are still essentially the same. It is because man can still recognize in them his own situation and religious experience that the Psalms appeal to people today. Outward details may vary, but if the God with whom the psalmists spoke is also the God of Jesus Christ, and if man's religious needs have not changed essentially since then, the Psalms still have a message for all Christians.

The Psalms and Comparative Religion

THE PICTURE that we have tried to draw of the religion of the Psalms has been based on an analysis of the psalms themselves, and we have only occasionally made use of material from comparative religion. While there is no doubt that the religious literature of the ancient Sumerians, Babylonians, and Egyptians contains much that is valuable for purposes of comparison with the biblical psalms, we have endeavored to let the Psalms of the Old Testament speak for themselves.

A comparison between the biblical and the nonbiblical psalms is, on the other hand, very instructive, both for the similarities and for the differences it reveals. It would bring us too far afield to establish here in detail the relationship between the psalms of Israel and, e.g., those of ancient Mesopotamia. But a few brief remarks might indicate some of the interesting insights that could be anticipated from such an investigation. We shall use to a great extent the findings of other students of the Psalms, but also draw attention to some matters frequently overlooked by Old Testament scholars.

Two things should be borne in mind on entering upon such a discussion. First, the same expression, when used in different religious literatures, does not always mean the same thing. Thus two similar phrases do not necessarily convey identical ideas. It is sufficient to recall the differing connotations of such words as "peace," "freedom," and "democracy" in the Western world and in Communist countries. Attention must therefore be paid to the whole religious and cultural environment in which an expression or a religious practice occurs. Second, the difference between biblical and non-biblical religion is not simply the difference between a profoundly spiritual religion and superficial and superstitious beliefs focusing on materialistic and selfish needs. The difference is much more subtle, and no generalization or over-simplification of this kind will lead to real understanding of the problem.

1) It is well known that there is a close formal affinity between the Babylonian and the Old Testament psalms. This is due primarily to the fact that the poetic canons were the same all over the ancient Near East, just as they are, to a great extent at least, throughout the Western world today. But there are also other points of resemblance. For instance, a psalm of lament is composed according to approximately the same pattern in Babylonia as in Israel. This pattern includes the following items: an invocation of God, lament with complaints of sickness and various evils, prayer for help and forgiveness, and a vow of thanksgiving (or formulas of gratitude).[1] We also find in the Babylonian psalms the same imagery to express the suffering of the psalmist: water and mire, grave and pit, wild beasts, et cetera. A few examples may show the surprising resemblance in wording:[2]

Babylonian	*Old Testament*
The wrath of god and goddess is placed upon me.	Thy wrath lies heavy upon me. *—Ps. 88:7*
How long, O my Lady, wilt thou be angry	How long, O Lord? Wilt thou forget me for ever?
and therefore thy face be turned away?	How long wilt thou hide thy face from me? *—Ps. 13:1*

116

Food I ate not, weeping was my bread, water I drank not, tears were my drink.

My tears have been my food, day and night. —*Ps. 42:3*

Friends and companions rage against me, the people of my city rage against me.

Even my bosom friend in whom I trusted, . . . has lifted his heel against me. —*Ps. 41:9*

He is thrown among the billows of the flood, the deluge has mounted over him, the shore is far off from him. . . he has perished in a deep place.

For the waters have come up to my neck. I sink in deep mire, where there is no foothold; I have come into deep waters, and the flood sweeps over me. —*Ps. 69:1,2*

Unloose my sin, loosen my iniquity. Remove my wantonness, loosen my transgression.

Pardon my guilt, for it is great.
. . . .
and forgive all my sins. —*Ps. 25:11,18*

This similarity in style and imagery might seem surprising at first sight. But it is understandable if we remember that the culture of the whole ancient Near East was relatively uniform and that these peoples shared the same scientific, or rather prescientific, conceptions of the world. It is to be expected that peoples sharing the same world view should in similar situations express their thoughts in similar words.

However, even from the purely stylistic point of view there is one striking difference between Israelitic and Sumerian-Babylonian psalmody. There is in the latter a tendency—not found in the biblical Psalms—toward monotony and tedious repetition, with names and epithets of gods being enumerated without adding anything new.

2) As regards religious content, the penitential psalms furnish some interesting comparative material. There are Babylonian psalms that contain confessions of sin, the sincerity of which cannot reasonably be questioned. (Strangely enough,

confession of sins is very rare in Egyptian religion.) By way of example, here is a prayer to the goddess Ishtar:

> I have cried to thee, suffering, wearied, and distressed, as
>   thy servant;
> See me, O my Lady, accept my prayers.
> Faithfully look upon me, and hear my supplication.
> Promise me forgiveness, and let thy spirit be appeased. . . .
> Forgive my sin, my iniquity, my shameful deeds, and my
>   offense,
> Overlook my shameful deeds, accept my prayer,
> Loosen my fetters, secure my deliverance, guide my steps
>   aright.[3] . . .

The following quotation from a "prayer to every god" is interesting in many respects, and reveals a fundamental difference between Israelitic and Babylonian religion. While there can be no doubt about the sincerity of the suppliant, he avows that he does not know all his sins—he may have transgressed some ritual prohibition without being aware of it—and he does not know against which god he has sinned:

> O Lord, my transgressions are many, great are my sins.
> O my god, my transgressions are many, great are my sins.
> O my goddess, my transgressions are many, great are my sins.
> The transgression which I have committed, indeed
>   I do not know.
> The sin which I have done, indeed I do not know.
> The forbidden thing which I have eaten, indeed
>   I do not know. . . .
> O my Lord, do not cast thy servant down;
> he is plunged into the waters of swamp, take his hand.
> The sin which I have done, turn into goodness,
> the transgression which I have committed, let the wind carry
>   away.[4] . . .

3) We have dealt with the religion of the Psalms as nourished by and expressed in the cult. Unfortunately, there exists no comparable study of Babylonian and Egyptian religion.[5] But it would seem that the cult played essentially the same

role there as it did in Israel. Here are a few selections from religious texts that illustrate this similarity:

> Verily, it is good always to walk behind Ishtar,
> it is good to walk behind her, the Mistress of Eanna.
> Before I walked regularly behind Ishtar,
> but went from house to house like a beggar
> and lay on the threshold like a dog,
> I had prickles in my foot and thorns in my garment.[6]

This man obviously had tried the service of several gods before he found that it was "good" to serve Ishtar in her temple and take part in her procession.

These selections are from inscriptions in Egyptian tombs:

> You have sacrificed. The gates are open.
> Received is that which you have offered.
> Your hands are pure at the act of the festival.
> Amon accepts it.
> He gives you life, health, and prosperity,
> and gladness of heart in royal favor
> for you in a beautiful [good] lifetime.
>
> How beautiful is the temple of Amon,
> all the day in feast with the divine King inside!
>
> O beautiful day when Amon's beauty is remembered!
> How glad is the heart!
> They sing praises before thee up to the skies.
> But our hearts are lifted up above all that we see.[7]

These quotations clearly indicate something of the psychological effects of the cult upon Babylonian and Egyptian worshipers.

4) Often quoted as an Egyptian parallel to an Old Testament psalm is the famous hymn to the sun of Pharaoh Akhenaton. It has, indeed, some remarkable points of similarity to Psalm 104. But there is one essential difference. Akhenaton describes how the sun god cares for all living creatures and gladdens man and beast with his light, but it is obvious that this takes place only in daytime; the night is a

period in which evil forces prevail until the appearance of the sun causes the dangers and fears of the night to disappear:

> When thou settest in the western horizon,
> the land is darkness, in the manner of death. . . .
> Every lion comes forth from his den;
> all creeping things, they sting.
> Darkness is a shroud, and the earth is stillness,
> for he who made them rests in the horizon.[8]

Now compare Psalm 104:

> Thou makest darkness, and it is night,
> when all the beasts of the forest creep forth.
> The young lions roar for their prey,
> seeking their food from God.
>
> *—Ps. 104:20,21*

Here the night too is part of God's creation. According to God's plan it fulfills a definite role in the economy of the world. "Thine is the day, thine also the night" (Ps. 74:16).

5) In the Egyptian temple of Horus at Edfu and in the temple of Hathor at Denderah there are some inscriptions—reminiscent of the so-called "entrance liturgies" in Psalms 15 and 24—which refer to the duties of the priests:

> O, you prophets and priests,
> all you who enter before the gods. . . .
> Do not appear with sin,
> do not enter in uncleanness,
> do not speak lies in his house!
> Do not embezzle the provisions!
> Do not collect taxes to the detriment of the
>   poor to benefit the rich!
> Do not add to the weight and the measure,
> but reduce them!
> Do not do wrong in matters of sacrifices![9]

In the sequel there is an even greater emphasis on cultic and ritual duties. There are obviously both ethical and cultic

requirements for those who enter the temple. But the emphasis on the cultic requirements is greater in Egypt than in
Israel.

6) Finally, attention should be drawn to a typically Israelitic passage from the Psalms:

> The idols of the nations are silver and gold,
> the work of men's hands.
> They have mouths, but they speak not,
> they have eyes, but they see not,
> they have ears, but they hear not,
> nor is there any breath in their mouths.
> Like them be those who make them!—
> yea, everyone who trusts in them!
>   —*Ps. 135:15-18*

Such an exclusiveness and such a contempt for other gods is
not to be found in the nonbiblical literature we have been
examining. A Babylonian psalmist can address his god in
terms such as these: "Who is like thee among the gods?" or
"Thou hast no equal." But he would never question the
existence or relative power of other gods. The exclusivism of
the Israelitic religion, on the other hand, is especially evident
in the hymns identified with the enthronement festival:

> For all the gods of the peoples are idols;
> but the Lord made the heavens.
> . . . .
> Say among the nations, "The Lord reigns!"
>   —*Ps. 96:5,10*

These ideas were most consistently expressed by the great
prophet of the exile, the so-called Second Isaiah (Isa., chaps.
40-55). It is significant that in numerous places this prophet
uses phrases and expressions that almost verbally agree with
the festival hymns. The psalms of the temple must have been
his inspiration.

Notes

INTRODUCTION

1. See especially H. Gunkel, *Einleitung in die Psalmen* (Göttingen, 1933).
2. S. Mowinckel, *Psalmenstudien,* II (Kristiania, 1921, reprinted 1960), and *Offersang og sangoffer* (Oslo, 1951).
3. S. Mowinckel, *Der achtundsechzigste Psalm* (Oslo, 1953).
4. Among these scholars are Hans Schmidt, *Die Psalmen* (Tübingen, 1934); F. M. T. Böhl, *Niewjaarsfest en Koningsdaag* (Groningen, 1927); Aage Bentzen, *Fortolkning til de gammeltestamentlige Salmer* (Copenhagen, 1939) ; and E. A. Leslie, *The Psalms* (New York: Abingdon-Cokesbury Press, 1949).
5. For an English introduction to the ideas of the Uppsala School see G. W. Anderson, *Harvard Theol. Review,* XLIII (1950), 239 ff. Cf. also A. Bentzen, *Theologische Rundschau,* XVII (1948-49), 273 ff.
6. *Interpreter's Bible* (New York: Abingdon Press, 1955), IV, 7.
7. A. Weiser, *Die Psalmen,* 5th ed. (Göttingen, 1959).
8. G. von Rad, *Das formgeschichtliche Problem des Hexateuchs* (Stuttgart, 1938), 32.
9. S. Mowinckel, *Zum israelitischen Neujahr* (Oslo, 1952), 46.
10. H.-J. Kraus, *Die Königsherrschaft Jahwes im Alten Testament* (Tübingen, 1951).
11. *Ibid.,* 23.
12. See, e.g., T. Säve-Söderbergh, *On Egyptian Representations of Hippopotamus Hunting* (Uppsala, 1953), 26.
13. H. Frankfort, *Kingship and the Gods* (Chicago: University of Chicago Press, 1948), 329.

14. A. R. Johnson in *The Old Testament and Modern Study*, H. H. Rowley, ed. (Oxford: Oxford University Press, 1952), 194 f.

15. Kraus, *op. cit.*, 145, footnote.

16. G. Quell, *Das Kultische Problem der Psalmen* (Stuttgart, 1936).

17. *Ibid.*, 8.

18. *Ibid.*, 10 f.

19. *Ibid.*, 18 ff.

20. The German *Frömmigkeit* (Swedish: *fromhet*) does not correspond exactly to the English "piety" and is also variously rendered by such other verbal equivalents as "religion," "living religion," "faith and piety," and simply "faith" (as in the title of this book).

CHAPTER 1

1. Cf. also Ps. 132:7 f., where mention is made of worshiping at the footstool of the Lord.

2. Or "crown" (Hebr., *miklal*).

3. Weiser, *op. cit.*, 19f., 32.

4. Kraus, *op. cit.*, 23.

5. Notice also in Ps. 63:1 the psalmist's thirst for God; cf. below p. 52.

6. See Harald Riesenfeld, *Jesus transfiguré* (Copenhagen, 1947), 97 ff.

7. Aage Bentzen, commenting on this passage in his *Fortolkning til de gammeltestamentlige Salmer,* points out that in Egyptian texts "seeing the beauty of the god" refers to seeing his statue in the temple or in a procession.

8. Johannes Pedersen, *Israel, Its Life and Culture* (London and Copenhagen, 1926-1940), III-IV, 451.

9. I.e., the courts of the temple.

10. The "river of thy delights" could also refer to the temple spring. The word "delights" (*'adanim*) reminds us of Eden ("delight"); and the spring, which bore the name of Gihon, seems to have had some symbolical connection with the river of paradise bearing the same name.

11. Cf. Ps. 28:2.

12. Or perhaps: This [my misery] shall I remember . . . when I go with the throng . . .

13. Notice that the expression "living God" recurs in Ps. 42:3.

14. Quell, *op. cit.*, 140.

15. J. Steinmann, *Les Psaumes* (Paris, 1951), 96 f.

16. A somewhat similar poem about the city of Memphis is found in an Egyptian papyrus; see Adolf Erman, *The Literature of the Egyptians* (London: Methuen, 1927), 205.

17. The word "elsewhere" is not in the Hebrew text. It is possible that a word has been lost here.

18. Pedersen, *op. cit.*, 351, mentions, in addition, Pss. 65:1; 76: 11; 107:22; 116:14 ff.

19. For the Old Testament idea of sacrifice, see Helmer Ringgren, *Sacrifice* (in the series World Christian Books, London, 1962).

20. Cf. H. H. Rowley's excellent discussion of similar passages in the prophets in *The Unity of the Bible* (Philadelphia: Westminster Press, 1953), 32 ff. (especially 39).

21. R. Dussaud, *Les origines cananéennes du sacrifice israélite,* 2nd ed. (Paris, 1941), 27 f.; Geo. Widengren, *The Accadian and Hebrew Psalms of Lamentation* (Uppsala, 1936), 31 f.

22. None of the psalms here quoted can be dated with any certainty in exilic or post-exilic times. Otherwise one might suppose that the destruction of the temple contributed to the spiritualization of sacrifices.

23. The verb means "to bind," with various shades of meaning; *chag* could be "dancing," "procession," "festival," or "festival sacrifice"; and finally *'abotim* can mean either "ropes" or "branches." But the translation "Bind the sacrifice with ropes" is less probable.

24. The Hebrew *hari'u* is from the same root as *teru'ah*, "joyful noise," "battle cry."

25. The day of the new moon (Ps. 81:4), the Feast of Tabernacles. E.g., Kissane, *The Book of Psalms* (Westminster, Maryland: Newman Press, 1953). Or the "covenant festival" (Bentzen *et al.* [?]).

26. Quell, *op. cit.,* 75 f.

27. Mowinckel, *Psalmenstudien,* II, 126 ff.; A. R. Johnson, *Sacral Kingship in Ancient Israel* (Cardiff, 1955), 78.

28. Notice the change of subject: ". . . *men* passed through . . . *we* rejoice." The worshipers regard themselves as present at the event.

29. Pedersen, *op. cit.,* I-II, 106 f.

30. Or "the day on which the Lord has acted."

31. The Hebrew *teru'ah*; cf. above note 24.

CHAPTER 2

1. Recent investigations of this topic include: J. de Fraine, *Biblica*, XXXI (1956), 324 ff., 445 ff.; and J. Scharbert, *Solidarität in Segen und Fluch im A. T.*, I (Bonn, 1958).

2. Cf. also vs. 3 of the same psalm: "Many will see and fear and put their trust in the Lord."

3. Significant in this connection are the role of the ark as the common sanctuary of the twelve tribes in premonarchic times, David's efforts to make Jerusalem the cultic center of his kingdom, and Jeroboam's concern to get new sanctuaries for the Northern Kingdom as soon as possible.

4. Otto J. Baab, *The Theology of the Old Testament* (New York: Abingdon, 1949), 59.

5. Cf. Pedersen, *op. cit.*, I-II, 264 f.

6. Another example is Ps. 38:11; cf. also Ps. 69:8, 26.

7. Weiser, *op. cit.*, 399.

8. Bentzen, *op. cit.*, 477.

9. Widengren, *Svensk exegetisk årsbok*, X (1945), 66 ff.

10. Intended is probably also a reference to the loneliness of the desert and the ruins.

CHAPTER 3

1. That the enemies are sorcerers is maintained by Mowinckel, *op. cit.*, I (Kristiania, 1921); that they are political enemies is asserted by H. Birkeland, *The Evildoers in the Psalms* (Oslo, 1955). A cogent discussion of the question is found in Widengren, *The Accadian and Hebrew Psalms of Lamentation*, 202 ff.

2. Whether this refers to a historical event or to a cultic reality is a matter of no great significance in this connection.

3. Cf. Widengren, *op. cit.*, 141.

4. See, e.g., N. M. Nicolsky, *Spuren magischer Formeln in den Psalmen* (Giessen, 1927).

5. Something similar can be said of Ps. 109:6-15 (notice also vss. 20 f.); cf. Steinmann, *Les Psaumes*, 123 ff.

6. Pedersen, *op. cit.*, I-II, 200.

7. *Ibid.*, 194 f.

8. The RSV is based on a Hebrew text that is probably not wholly correct. Read *li hadar wa'oz* instead of *leharri 'oz*. For the combination, cf. Prov. 31:25 (Kissane).

9. Literally "sons of man," or simply "human beings."

10. Literally "sons of male," which could also be a synonym of "sons of man." In that case the two expressions would be nothing but poetical variations of the same concept—human beings.

11. Cf. the attitude of the Assyrian king according to Isa. 10: 7-11, 13-14 and the prophet's judgment in reaction to it, vss. 15 ff.

CHAPTER 4

1. For more detailed studies of these terms see L. Gulkowitsch, *Die Entwicklung des Begriffes Hasid im A. T.* (Tartu, 1934); A. R. Johnson, "Hesed and hasid" in *Interpretationes* (Mowinckel jubilee volume, Oslo, 1955), 100 ff.; H. A. Brongers on *hasid* in *Nederlands Theologisch Tijdschrift*, 1954, 279 ff.; H. Birkeland, *'ani und 'anaw in den Psalmen* (Oslo, 1933); Mowinckel, *Psalmenstudien*, I (on "the evildoers").

2. Ivan Engnell in *Svenskt bibliskt uppslagsverk* (Gävle-Stockholm, 1948-52), II, 1420.

3. Cf. II Chron. 6:41, where "priests" and "saints" are probably the priests and the congregation.

4. The situation is similar in the few examples of the use of this term outside the Psalms: in Micah 7:2 it is parallel to "upright"; in Isa. 57:1 "men of *chesed*" (RSV: "devout men") is more or less equivalent to "the righteous"; and in Prov. 20:6 "man of loyalty" and "faithful man" are parallel expressions.

5. Thus Birkeland, *'ani und 'anaw in den Psalmen.*

6. J. van der Ploeg, *Oudtestamentische Studiën,* VII (Leiden, 1950), 236 ff.

7. The translation of this line and the next is uncertain.

8. Mowinckel, *op. cit.*

9. Widengren, *The Accadian and Hebrew Psalms of Lamentation,* 197 ff.

10. Birkeland, *The Evildoers in the Psalms.*

11. H. Ringgren, *Vetus Testamentum,* III (1953), 265 ff.; T. Worden, *ibid.,* III, 284; Roger T. O'Callaghan, *ibid.,* IV (1954), 169.

12. Engnell, *Svenskt bibliskt uppslagsverk,* II, 827 f.

13. Pedersen, *op. cit.,* 453-496.

CHAPTER 5

1. This whole section can also be translated as a statement: God arises, his enemies are scattered, et cetera.

2. Notice in this connection Ps. 130:4: "There is forgiveness with thee, that thou mayest be feared." Other references to "fear" of God are: Pss. 52:6; 64:9 f.; 102:15; 48:5 f. Note also *pachad,* "fear, dread," in Ps. 36:1 and Ps. 119:120.

3. The futility of the idols is even expressed in the word that is used, *elil,* which is curiously like *el,* "God."

4. And this line is absent from the parallel version of this psalm in II Sam. 22:21.

5. "Shadow of death" is a late and secondary interpretation. The reference is primarily to narrow and dark valleys, where wild beasts and robbers have their haunts. In a few cases, however, the word is used with reference to Sheol.

6. Cf. Ps. 56:4 and Ps. 118:6.

7. "Rock" is simply a symbol of stability and strength, although some scholars have thought to detect other allusions in the term.

8. This interpretation makes the image immediately intelligible. But it is not improbable that it originally had something to do with the temple, where the wings of the cherubs overshadowed the ark of the covenant. This would explain why, in Ps. 61:4, "under the shelter of thy wings" is parallel to "in thy tent."

9. Or possibly, with the ancient versions, "seize" or "hold."

10. Cf. also Ps. 25:5, "Lead me in thy truth, and teach me . . . for thee I wait."

11. H. J. Franken, *The Mystical Communion with YHWH in the Book of Psalms* (Leiden, 1954).

12. The word *siach* can even sometimes mean "to lament" or "to speak."

13. Franken, *op. cit.,* 21.

14. *Ibid.,* 34.

15. Cf. A. Neher, *L'essence du prophétisme* (Paris, 1955), 255 f.

16. Bentzen, *op. cit.,* p. 132, and Franken, *op. cit.,* 41 f.

17. Neher, *op. cit.,* 261.

CHAPTER 6

1. Franken, *op. cit.,* 59 ff.

2. *Ibid.,* 60.

3. *Ibid.,* 61.

4. *Ibid.,* 62.

5. *Ibid.,* 63.

6. Widengren, *Svensk exegetisk årsbok,* X (1945), 66 ff.

7. The parallel version, II Sam. 22:5, has "waves of death," which might be preferable.

8. See below in the Appendix, pp. 116 ff.

9. I.e., kinsmen.

10. Other instances include: Pss. 25:18; 31:10 (Hebrew text); 40:12; 41:4; and 107:17.

11. H. H. Rowley in *The Unity of the Bible*, 39, reminds us that we should not "approach the Bible in the spirit of a lawyer arguing the meaning of an Act of Parliament." Unfortunately, this principle is too often forgotten!

12. There is no reason to change the text, as the RSV does.

13. Widengren, *The Accadian and Hebrew Psalms of Lamentation*, 156, 187.

14. A word from the same root occurs in Ps. 26:4, where it is rendered "dissemblers."

15. H. Schmidt, *Das Gebet der Angeklagten im Alten Testament* (Giessen, 1928).

16. See above, p. 44.

17. Cf. above, p. 59.

CHAPTER 7

1. We have intimated above (p. 69) that Ps. 51:8 could allude to such an oracle; there might be another such allusion in Ps. 85:8, "Let me hear what God the Lord will speak, for he will speak peace to his people."

2. Cf. Claus Westermann, *Das Loben Gottes in den Psalmen* (Göttingen, 1954), 53: "The praise is not a substitute for sacrifice, but has an original significance of its own. The sacrifice is food for the god, but praise belongs as much to the life of the god as does food." It should, however, be kept in mind that *todah* means both "thanksgiving" and "sacrifice of thanksgiving."

3. Cf. Westermann, *op. cit.*, 18 f.

4. Weiser, *op. cit.*, 58.

5. Westermann makes the same point, *op. cit.*, 20 f.

6. Cf. Westermann, *op. cit.*, 19.

7. *Ibid.*, 17.

8. *Ibid.*, 21. Westermann's distinction is accepted by several German scholars.

9. "Upon the whole blessings must be mutual. . . . Also the lesser people may, according to their humble means, bless the

great. Thus they confirm the blessing which the great actually possess, and thus they contribute to its increase." Pedersen, *op. cit.,* 203. "Yahweh is exalted above all blessing, it is said. . . . This [implies] that he cannot be blessed enough. His claim to blessing is so great, because all blessing is concentrated in him." *Ibid.,* 204.

10. Westermann, *op. cit.,* 54 f.
11. The "gates" and "courts" are those of the temple.
12. Thus also Ps. 135:1, 2.
13. Other similar examples are Pss. 57:9,10 = 108:3,4; 107:1; 117; 136:1.
14. Cf. Westermann, *op. cit.,* 77.
15. This section is a variant version of Ps. 135:8-12, with the recurring refrain "for his steadfast love endures for ever."
16. Or "and not we [ourselves]."

CHAPTER 8

1. See above, pp. xv ff.
2. See above, p. xiii.
3. A recent paper on this topic by G. Widengren is found in *Culture in History* (Essays in honor of Paul Radin), Stanley Diamond, ed. (New York: Columbia University Press, 1960), 467 ff.
4. See, e.g., S. H. Hooke, *Myth and Ritual* (Oxford, 1933), 3 f., *In the Beginning,* The Clarendon Bible, VI (Oxford, 1948), 18.
5. Or perhaps, "the deep covered it like a garment."
6. Cf. Bentzen's commentary on this psalm.
7. See above, p. 14.
8. Although Deuteronomy appears as a speech of Moses, it is obvious that it reflects the cultic preaching of the (late) monarchic period; cf. G. von Rad, *Studies in Deuteronomy* (Naperville, Allenson, 1953).
9. Is this psalm historical or cultic? For a cultic interpretation, in which interesting Babylonian parallels are cited, see F. Willesen, *Vetus Testamentum,* II (1952), 289 ff.
10. Ringgren, *Teologisk Tidskrift/Teologinen Aikakauskirja* (Helsinki, 1948), LIII, 237 f.
11. A monograph on this psalm has been published in the German language by G. W. Ahlström, *Psalm 89* (Lund, 1959).
12. A similar idea is perhaps intended in Ps. 8:2, "a bulwark because of thy foes, to still the enemy and the avenger." See Bentzen's commentary.

13. See above, p. 16.

14. Something similar is found in Egypt, when one Pharaoh after another enumerates the same peoples and cities that he has conquered. The enumeration has become a traditional pattern that is repeated even if it does not reflect the actual historical situation.

CHAPTER 9

1. The translation is uncertain. There seems to be an allusion to a similar phrase in the commandment, "You shall not take the name of the Lord your God in vain."

2. See G. Östborn, *Tora in the Old Testament* (Lund, 1945), ch. 1, and I. Engnell, *Israel and the Law,* 2nd ed. (Uppsala, 1954).

3. I. Engnell, in *Studia orientalia J. Pedersen dedicata* (Copenhagen, 1953).

4. Or "your throne, O god," making the king a "divine" being.

5. For a fuller treatment of these questions, see Helmer Ringgren, *The Messiah in the Old Testament,* 2nd ed. (London, 1961).

APPENDIX

1. The pattern has been worked out by Widengren in *The Accadian and Hebrew Psalms of Lamentation.*

2. The examples are taken from Widengren, *op. cit.* 37, 95-135, 258-274.

3. J. B. Pritchard, ed., *Ancient Near Eastern texts,* rev. ed. (Princeton: Princeton University Press, 1955), 384 f.

4. Ibid. 391 f.

5. Some relevant observations in this connection with respect to Egypt are to be found in S. Morenz, *Ägyptische Religion* (Stuttgart, 1960), 85 ff.

6. Erich Ebeling, *Literarische Keilschrifte aus Assur* (Berlin, 1953), No. 29d, lines 8 ff.; see *Bibliotheca orientalis,* XIV (1956), 114.

7. Siegfried Schott, *Altägyptische Festdaten* (Wiesbaden, 1950), 74. Other examples are to be found in Charles G. Cumming, *The Assyrian and Hebrew Hymns of Praise* (New York: Columbia University Press, 1934), 112 f., Maurice Brillant and René Aigrain, *Histoire des religions,* III (Paris, 1955), 77 ff.

8. Pritchard, *op. cit.,* 370 f.

9. R. Alliot, *Le culte d'Horus à Edfou,* I (Cairo, 1949), 184 f.

Indexes

TOPICAL INDEX

INDEX OF BIBLICAL PASSAGES

110:1, 2–113	118:28, 29–81	139:14–97
111:5, 6–42	119–57, 112	139:16–97
112:9–41	122–xviii, 9	139:21, 22–30
113:7–41	122:1–3	139:23, 24–56
115:1-3–31	127:1, 2–32	141:2–12
116:1–51	128:5–33	142:7–80
116:3–39	129:23, 24–55	143:5–57
116:8, 9–39, 74	130:4–71	145:5–57
116:13–15	130:5, 6–52	146:3–34
116:15–39	132–xvii	147:1–82
116:17–12	132:13-14–1	147:15-18–104
118:1–81, 82	132:15–41	147:19, 20–104
118:6-7–34	134:2, 3–79	148–92
118:15–92	134:3–33	148:5, 6–86
118:17, 18–74	135:3-5–88	148:6–96
118:21–81	135:6-10, 12–103	148:14–39
118:24–17	135:15-18–121	149:1, 2, 4–39
118:26–33	136:1 ff.–88	149:3–14
118:27–13	139:7-10–55	150:1–81

Type used in this book
Body, 11 on 13 and 10 on 11 Baskerville
Display, Baskerville
Paper: G. M. Standard Antique